RETIREMENT REBOOT

Dennis Miller

CONTENTS

Chapter 1
The Road We Traveled   4

Chapter 2
I Feel Like I'm Trying to Drink from a Fire Hose   14

Chapter 3
Just What, Exactly, is the Problem?   26

Chapter 4
It is Time to Get Started   41

Chapter 5
There are Lots of Folks Who Want to Help   51

Chapter 6
Taking the Plunge! 66

Chapter 7
Using Good Resources 81

Chapter 8
These Baby Shoes are Made for Walking 92

Chapter 9
The Offshore Decision 107

Chapter 10
Wrapping Things Up 126

Chapter 1

THE ROAD WE TRAVELED

Like many folks who subscribe to investment newsletters, my wife and I took a pretty good hit when the housing market crashed in 2008. We're seniors, and we're no longer working. We don't have money from a job to help us to make up for our losses. Our challenge is: How do we take what we have accumulated over our lifetimes, pay for a decent standard of living, and then, hopefully, be lucky enough to pass something along to our children?

Inflation is working against us. According to Shadowstats.com, the true inflation rate is already over 7%. It's likely to go much higher, so if we do nothing about it, the eventual losses in the buying power of our life savings could make the 2008 losses look pale by comparison.

Over the last several years I've corresponded with the authors of quite a few newsletters, asking for advice and clarification and sometimes offering them suggestions on how they might go about delivering their points to senior citizens a bit better, in a language we could all understand and relate to. It was during one of those exchanges that David Galland from Casey Research put forth a challenge. Here is what he tossed me:

"When a person decides to get informed about this stuff, it quickly becomes overwhelming. Do they buy bullion, gold or silver, GLD [an exchange-traded fund specializing in gold] or avoid GLD like the plague, is the government suppressing

gold or not, what about gold stocks (big or small), and if gold stocks, who do you listen to (one guy says he's a good guy, but others say he's a crook), is EverBank safe (Weiss may have a different opinion), is the US dollar going to be the winner if the euro crashes, or will the euro persevere because the ECB [European Central Bank] has so far refused to print, will the government confiscate, or not?

"Ah, the hell with it, just call the whole thing off – it's simpler just to roll over my CD!

"It's a real issue – we are all running so fast, and so far ahead, that we forget that others are trying to gingerly pull into traffic, and getting run over.

"Dennis, you like to write, maybe you should do some 'Here's how to get started' type content?"

Before I go on, let me add something that has happened. As discussions with David progressed, he mentioned that Casey Research has some of the best financial editors in the business. I am now totally convinced of that.

At the same time, intuitively I felt that I wanted to share my experiences with the kind of everyday folks who are our peer group, including my own circle of friends. The kind of folks I am talking about may well have owned a local dry cleaner, sold insurance, taught school, *etc.* Most of us did well enough at accumulating wealth, but we weren't economists or what I would term "savvy" investors in the stock market, so we generally delegated investment decisions to others.

5

At this point in our lives, my wife and I have investments in many places. But we don't just "have" them. More important to us is that we **understand** them. After a lot of hard work and thinking, we chose them as the best way to protect ourselves not only from inflation but from what many call hyperinflation, which seems to be looming on the horizon. Indeed, we are very concerned about our future, the future of this country, and protecting our life savings.

STARTING AT "VERY BAD"

The experience of rearranging our investments to get the protection we believed we needed mirrored something I had done before, although that earlier experience had nothing to do with money.

Several years ago my career demanded that I spend 40+ weeks a year on the road, eating out in nice restaurants with clients almost every night. My body didn't hide the fact that it had been neglected for quite some time. One of my clients gave me a book on physical conditioning. It was written by a runner and was a primer on how to get your body into some kind of decent shape.

The premise was pretty easy. You start by taking a test – see how far you can walk or run in 12 minutes. You then take that distance and look on a chart in the book to find the category you're in. Then you go to the matching chapter, and that's where you begin your conditioning program.

I was pumped up, took off for my 12 minutes, noted the distance, and found that I was in the category titled "Very Bad." I read that particular chapter, worked diligently for an entire month, then took the test again. The distance I traveled was a good bit more. I was excited, and I went to see what category I was in and discovered I had made it up to "Poor." At that point, I didn't know whether to cheer or cry. But I stuck with it, and after a year or so I could actually run three miles without stopping. I was still a long, long way from those who run the marathons, but it certainly put me ahead of many in my age group.

ENTER GRANDMA

As I look back, I can see that as an investor, I've followed a pretty similar path. "Very bad" would have been an appropriate rating of my investment knowledge not too many years ago. Now I've progressed to where I may be ahead of many in what I've learned, but at the same time a long way from those who stand at the podium or sit behind a computer screen, offering others detailed investment advice.

I believed for several years that to really make changes and improve your skill in almost anything, two ingredients are needed: motivation and education. The initial motivation for learning about investments was actually thrust upon me. It happened 25 years ago, shortly after my wife and I married.

My father-in-law passed away, the family homestead in Indiana was auctioned off, and my mother-in-law, whom I affectionately referred to as "Grandma," moved in less than a mile from us in Florida. Grandma took the money from the sale and put it in her checking account. That was the only place she had to deposit the funds. Of course, we piped up and told her that she was over the amount the Federal Deposit Insurance Corporation (FDIC) would insure and that she really needed to get some of the money out of the bank.

At the time my wife and I had an investment account at a major brokerage firm, likely with around $10,000 in it. A neighbor I had met at our community pool was our stockbroker, and he had helped me open up the account. Then he left the firm, and our account was turned over to a nice lady who invited us out to lunch. Sometimes I wonder if we are the only people who were so casual about selecting the person who would help look after our life savings.

It didn't take long for the family to decide that, because we lived the closest to Grandma, we would have the responsibility for helping look after her investments. We had a big meeting in the conference room of the brokerage firm. Grandma wrote a big check to them, and my wife and I signed the documents that gave us power of attorney to look after her investments. I will never forget looking at the number on the bottom of Grandma's first statement. It seemed huge to me at the time, and I felt frightened. I had never looked after that much money before.

My motivation to get it right was further enhanced by one of those looks only your spouse can give and which sends a message without uttering a word. It was as though she had a red neon sign on her forehead that flashed, "Don't you dare lose mother's money!" And that is where our personal journey began.

Knowing that "motivation by itself energizes incompetence," I attacked the problem from two different angles. I needed a whole lot of education to meld with my motivation. The first route was to learn as much as I could from the "nice lady" who was our broker. The second was to sign up for many newsletters, read several books, and begin to get educated on how to invest and not lose Grandma's money.

CD SOLUTION

Over the next several years, with the help of the investment newsletters and books and the broker guiding us along the way, we invested in stocks and other vehicles. Some were winners – and a couple were big winners – but many were not winners at all. After about three years of this, I did some analysis. I concluded that if we had taken Grandma's money and invested it in 6% certificates of deposits (CDs), there would have been more money in her account, and life would have been much less stressful for all of us. So we started moving money into CDs.

While the broker was supportive and showed us how to get better CD rates through a brokerage firm than by shopping for them locally, I'm sure she took a good hit on lost commissions, because we were no longer buying and selling stocks regularly. Grandma lived for almost 20 years after we started handling her finances, and when all the chips were counted, the family was pleased at the job we had done. We hadn't lost Grandma's money.

During that time, my wife and I saw our own investment accounts grow as well. At first I was buying and selling stocks regularly, but with similar mediocre results as we had with Grandma's account. Years later I read a blurb in a Casey newsletter that described me perfectly. We would have a gain and sell much too quickly, so that we could say we made a profit – but only a small one. If the investment went down, panic would be the result, and again we would sell quickly. I guess that somewhere during that period my investment grade went from "very bad" to "poor."

In the middle of that process, the nice lady retired, which was a blessing and a curse at the same time. We decided to move the accounts to Charles Schwab, where we could manage the money ourselves, with lower trading fees. And everything could easily be handled by computer. We knew how to find the best CDs on the website and did not need a broker to help us.

Then we just stopped renewing our investment-newsletter subscriptions. We took the money my wife inherited, plus what we had accumulated over 20 years, and put the money in CDs – some paying as much as 7% interest – and moved on.

Managing that portfolio was easy. Every time a CD matured, we would buy another one that went out a few years. It probably took less than three hours a year of real work. Each year we spent less than the total interest, so the account always had more in it at year end than the year before. We figured we were set for life. Little did we know that our dream world was going to come crashing down, taking less than 90 days to do so.

A NEW WORLD ARRIVES

It was the fall of 2008 when the real estate market crashed and the government decided to pass the Troubled Assets Relief Program (TARP) Bill to bail out the banks that were "too big to fail." The idea was that the banks would pump the money into the economy and it would immediately turn around.

Right away, I realized that my wife and I had a huge problem. The banks never lent that money out into the economy; they used it to pay off their own debt. In a three-month period, we had over half of our CDs called in by the banks; the juicy ones with the 6% coupons were the first to go. We had one at 7% with five years remaining that also got called in pretty quickly. Our first reaction was to do what we had done in the past – start shopping for more CDs to roll the money into. **Uh oh!** The best rate we could get was 2% interest. We were panicked, because we realized that our retirement dreams would be crushed as we took a two-thirds cut in income.

We had to do something different to survive, and pretty quickly. Talk about motivation; being scared to death is a pretty good motivator. Somehow I had a feeling in the pit of my stomach that something wasn't right, that something was different. The education I needed – and needed quickly – would be much different than what we learned when we started looking after Grandma's money.

In our next chapter I'll tell you about the steps we took to get back on track – who we called, what we did, and how we got to where we are today. And I'll 'fess up to the mistakes we made along the way. Little did we know when we started that three years later we would have money invested in seven different currencies, CDs that are denominated in foreign money *and* that are FDIC insured, multiple forms of gold and silver, ETF shares, speculative gold stocks, and accounts in other countries. But that's how we found a way to sleep at night, knowing we have done a whole lot to protect ourselves.

From what do we feel we must protect ourselves? The turmoil of hyperinflation, which is looming large on the investment horizon.

I would urge all reading this book to stop and take a step back for a moment. Generally, all of the events I have outlined were a result of something happening and my wife and I having to react. Most folks would likely agree that the investors who have the most success are the ones who see and react ahead of the crowd when market fundamentals are changing. Somehow they mentally switch from "reactive" to "strategic" mode and develop a new or modified investment strategy to deal with what they see ahead on the horizon. I would suggest to every reader, before moving on to the next chapter, to ask yourself three questions:

1. What do you see on the horizon for our country and economy?

2. If you had to develop an investment strategy to protect yourself from what you think is coming, what would the strategy be?

3. Considering the way you are currently invested, are the items now in your investment accounts the best preparation for what lies ahead?

If the answer to #3 is "No," then you must ask one more question:

Can you afford to wait, or are you better off making some changes? Those who spot the trends and invest ahead of the crowd generally seem to do a whole lot better than those who wait and follow the crowd.

Our road wasn't straight. It had lots of bumps, and many times we took the wrong fork and had to backtrack. I truly believe we still have a lot of road in front of us. Try as we might, we cannot see clearly over the crest in front of us, so all we can do is try to prepare for the twists, turns, hills, and potholes that are still going to have to be navigated. But as David Galland suggested in his email, just maybe I can help some others along the path, and hopefully they can learn from some of my mistakes. Stay tuned.

Chapter 2

I FEEL LIKE I'M TRYING TO DRINK FROM A FIRE HOSE

Part of David Galland's challenge to me was to put together a step-by-step report on how to get started preparing yourself for the possibility of hyperinflation.

My initial thought was that the first step was the easiest one to identify but possibly the toughest one to implement. Let me explain.

Imagine sitting down with your morning coffee, turning on your computer, opening up the link to your brokerage account, and discovering that your cash balance was well over 20 times what it was the day before. Your reaction would be something like "My God, what is going on?" But that's exactly how one of my days started three years ago.

After my initial shock, I clicked on "Account History" and saw that several of our CDs had been called in all at once in the middle of the night. It took me a few minutes to realize what was going on and then come to grips with the fact that I might have seen just the tip of the iceberg.

I went to the web page where I shopped CDs to see what was available to replace the ones that had been called in. I found several that were available – if I'd take a 2% yield and if I were willing to commit our money for ten years. And there were a couple of so-called bargains, should I only want to go out seven years. That's when it struck me: We were about to take a huge income hit with no easy way to remedy the situation. I'm sure my face was red, and I was beginning to panic.

Most folks have heard the saying that with age comes wisdom, and maybe that's true. I was approaching 70 years old at the time and had finally learned that if you are in crisis mode and then panic, your knee-jerk reaction is usually not too smart. The folks who fare well in life seem to be able to hold panic under control while they gain some perspective on the problem that's threatening them. They make better choices to deal with the situation, even when the situation looks bad.

At that same time that all the CD money came home without calling ahead, I got really lucky. Recall that this was the last quarter of 2008, right after the presidential election. The morning paper had an article focusing on perspective. It noted how the election seemed to polarize the country, and that folks who were for or against the president-elect really had some strong feelings about it. He then pleaded for perspective, pointing out that if the person you voted for won the election, likely you would be quite excited. He then went on to say that history has proven that things never turn out quite as well for the winners as they had hoped. And if the person you voted for lost, things never turn out quite as bad as you feared. Boy, the timing of that message was a blessing for me.

I thought it through, and it really applied to our situation. My wildest fears were that we would have to immediately sell the house, downsize, and change our standard of living radically. After reading the article, a little voice in my head told me to calm down, relax, take a deep breath, and reassess the situation. Okay, that makes sense. Realistically we were not broke. As a matter of fact, our brokerage account probably had its highest cash balance ever. What had really happened is that we sold what had been a good investment, now had cash, and needed to find other investments that would help us maintain our standard of living.

GETTING A GRIP

Then I did the worst-case scenario, checking to see how much cash we would have if the rest of the CDs were called in by tomorrow morning. I took that amount, divided it by what we spent the previous year, and came to the conclusion that if we kept it all in cash, with zero percent interest, we were okay for over a decade. I had always believed that to have enough money for retirement you should be able to live off the interest and not touch the principal. But should we have to go into the principal, we certainly had plenty of time to adjust our standard of living. Time for me to get a grip!

As an aside, after the first two days the call-in pattern changed. The bank would wait until the next interest payment was due, pay it, and at the same time call in the CD. After the first full year, only three CDs hadn't been called in by the bank. I then called the Schwab bond department and sold them for a premium over par. Today – three years later – we do not own any CDs denominated in US dollars.

So the first step is the easy one to explain, but it can be difficult to take. That is, *calm down, take a deep breath, the world is not coming to an end, fight the panic, and try to draw a realistic perspective.* I have to say that was tough for me at first, but once I was able to cope with the situation realistically, the next steps became clear. I needed help, and I started to make a list of whom I should call.

I went into my center desk drawer to get the four stacks of business cards I had accumulated over my working career. I picked up two of the stacks, and the rubber bands were so dried out they just crumbled. When I sorted through the cards, I came up with four people whom I thought I could go to for advice: my old stockbroker, who really was a good friend and very knowledgeable; a couple of friends who I knew to be good investors; and Glen Kirsch (sad to say he has since passed away) of Asset Strategies International (ASI). The last time I had spoken to Glen was January 1997, when I bought some gold from ASI.

INFLATION WORRY DAWNS

Before I phoned anyone, it made sense to me to write down a few questions. Something was bothering me also. I'm not an economist, although I took Business Economics I & II in college several decades ago. About the only thing I remembered was that the professor kept making examples of guns and butter, and as a 20-year-old kid I never could connect how that related to the real world.

My thought process was this: We were in the last quarter of 2008, President Obama was then president-elect, and the Bush term was winding down. The federal budget deficit went above $500 billion;

then they passed the TARP Bill that would add another $500 billion to the total. The incoming president was already discussing an additional huge bailout package, and they were also making it known there would be a massive new government-spending program. In my lifetime I had never seen that type of full-throttle deficit spending. Isn't that the kind of stuff that causes really high inflation? I remember all too well the Jimmy Carter years, when inflation got close to 20% and no one could sell their house because mortgage interest rates were something like 18%.

As I put together my questions, the first had nothing to do with where we should invest our cash, but rather was what I termed "a sanity check." With all the things going on, with the government spending so much money it didn't have, is the logical result that down the road we would have inflation like we did in the Jimmy Carter era? Each one of the four folks I spoke with said, **"Absolutely!"**

From that point, the discussion went to how does a senior citizen, no longer working, find a way to protect himself from the ravages of inflation? At the end of the day I remarked that a week ago I would have thought rolling a CD into another one at 6% would be a good investment, but now I realize that with high inflation coming, we are go to have to do a whole lot better than that just to stay even, much less stay ahead of the game.

MUCH TO LEARN

Glen Kirsch was the only one of the four who was still working, and he specialized in helping folks like myself protect their assets. Our first conversation ran well over an hour, and over the next two weeks we spent many more hours discussing what had to be done and how to do it.

He told me about investment ideas most people still have never heard of.

- Perth Mint Certificates

- How to move my IRA offshore legally

- Managed accounts with Weber Hartman Vrijhof & Partners (WHVP) in Zurich

- Investing in foreign currencies

- The pluses and minuses of exchange-traded funds (ETFs)

- How much hard metal I should have versus stocks

- What percentage should be "core holdings"

- How much should be hedge investments against inflation

- How much do I want to hold outside the country in case the government decides to call in all the gold like Roosevelt did

At the time I knew Roosevelt had done something about gold. What I did not know was that he called in all the gold and paid the citizens $20/oz. for it. Once he had all the gold, he then arbitrarily revalued it to $35/oz. Glen helped me understand that the $15 revision was the same as devaluing the currency in everyone's pocket by 75% ($15 being 75% of $20). We discussed gold and silver stocks – not particular companies, but the difference between owning speculative stocks versus big companies. My head was spinning. I mentioned to Glen that I felt like I was trying to drink from a fire hose. Indeed, I was overwhelmed.

Glen then sent me a load of material that took several hours to read, and the more I read, the longer the list of questions grew. We exchanged several emails. I even tried to draw up a flow chart to see if I finally understood what he was trying to tell me. A couple of my messages came back with a note saying "not exactly," which I'll admit fed my frustration. Glen was one of the most patient people I had ever met, and he stuck with me all the way, although inside he had to be getting as frustrated as I was. He also told me to rejoin an organization called Sovereign Society and named a few other newsletters I should sign up for. I did sign up and soon found my inbox flooded with a whole lot more reading material.

Shortly after that, I was reading Chuck Butler and the *Currency Capitalist*. It offered a home-study course on trading currencies on the foreign exchange (forex) market. The forex market is similar to the stock market but with an important difference: currencies are traded against one another. Daily trading volume in the forex market is much higher than on the New York Stock Exchange. I took the course, not necessarily with the intention of trading currencies, but rather to understand what makes one currency rise and another go down.

The email I'd received from David Galland three years later was right on target. Things are so complicated that folks get overwhelmed. It's much easier for them to just roll over their CDs. As I look back, had we owned a diversified stock portfolio instead of being totally invested in CDs, more than likely I too would have thrown my hands up in despair at understanding the new world I had stepped into.

Luckily for me the folks I talked to helped me realize that stocks and most all investments denominated in US dollars could be vulnerable to high inflation. Glen convinced me that I really needed to educate myself into a whole new way of thinking about investing. I asked him why I couldn't just find a good certified financial planner (CFP). His response was that in the US very few if any CFPs "get it" and understand the problem. Once I started working with the WHVP folks in Zurich, I would quickly understand what he meant. Three years later, I have to agree with Glen.

MORE THAN A JIMMY CARTER PROBLEM

As I look back, I now know that even though I thought I understood the problem, I really didn't. I was worried about Jimmy Carter type inflation. After taking up David Galland's invitation to attend a Casey/Sprott conference in Phoenix about *When Money Dies*, I realized that the problems facing most investors today are much greater than anything in the 1970s.

Doug Casey was the keynote speaker at the conference, and he put up a chart showing the federal deficits and then the liabilities, both funded and unfunded. He challenged his staff to find any type of reasonable scenario where the US could come out of this bind without serious inflation and currency devaluation... and his final conclusion was, "We're screwed!"

Shortly after I got home from the conference, Ed Steer in his *Gold and Silver Daily* posted a graph from the FDIC titled "Stash the Cash." It showed how rapidly the amount of bank deposits in the economy has been rising. According to the FDIC, in the year 2000, deposits at US banks totaled $4 trillion. In 2010 they reached $10 trillion. Isn't a huge, rapid increase in the money supply what caused hyperinflation in Germany,

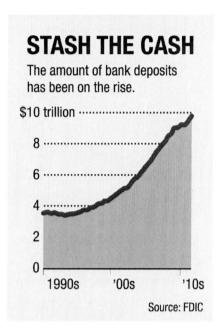

STASH THE CASH

The amount of bank deposits has been on the rise.

Source: FDIC

Yugoslavia, Argentina, and Zimbabwe? For me, the motivation element for changing my investment strategy was well supplied, so it was time to get to the education part. I knew that no one would look after our life savings with the same intensity as my wife and I would, so I told myself, "Let's get on with it."

Recently I read an article written a few years back by Bud Conrad, the chief economist at Casey Research. Here is what he had to say on inflation:

"Government debt makes inflation attractive for politicians. Inflation is a slow-motion default – a default on the installment plan."

At the Casey/Sprott conference, many speakers put up charts showing things like growing government debt, the rising supply of newly created cash, and inflation rates for countries that went through hyperinflation. In all cases, the charts showed an upward trend line and then at some point the line went straight up. My conclusion was that if inflation is slow-motion default, then hyperinflation is default at the speed of light. The economic and social chaos it would cause is difficult to fathom.

After much reading and talking with newsletter writers and other investment professionals, I came up with a list of the types of investments that historically have protected people from the ravages of inflation. I am sure some readers have longer lists, but ours began with "true assets" – gold, silver, and farmland, to be specific. In addition, one might consider certain stocks, both large company and speculative, in the metals industry and perhaps energy stocks. It seems likely that the price of oil would rise with inflation.

Next on the list were currencies, which get even more complicated. Not only did it include owning the currency, but also ETFs tied to foreign currencies, stocks on foreign stock exchanges, and bonds of certain foreign governments. As an example, Nestlé is a household name, but it is a Swiss company. One of our current holdings is a Nestlé 6% corporate bond denominated in Australian dollars.

THE TIME IS NOW

I have a friend who says, "Why make a decision today if it can be put off until tomorrow?" While that might sound cute, waiting until the transmission on your car is totally broken and having the vehicle towed to a dealer for a trade-in certainly isn't the optimal way to negotiate the price of a new vehicle. You can't drive around and shop at other dealers to get a decent price. Unfortunately, this is the way he has lived his life. The more difficult the decision is financially or emotionally, the longer he drags his feet. What he has yet to understand is that doing nothing is also a decision and can turn out to be very, very expensive.

If you don't want to follow in my friend's footsteps, I have three suggestions:

1. When you see storm clouds on the investment horizon, don't ignore them and hope they will go away. Ask any Floridian who has walked outside during the calm of the eye of a hurricane, and they will tell you it is quite peaceful, yet the storm clouds are clearly in sight. In a matter of minutes it can go from calm to absolutely terrifying, since the strongest winds are closest to the eye.

2. Many decisions in life are difficult both financially and emotionally. I have come to believe one is better off by "fighting the panic and trying to draw a realistic perspective."

3. There is an old saying, "When the student is ready to learn, the teacher shall appear." It is unrealistic to think that when we see there is a problem (certainly protecting

our life savings would fall into that category), we should immediately have all the answers. Seek help from folks who may have been down the road before you. Don't be shy about contacting a number of people you respect. You will likely find – as I did – that many folks are glad to share their knowledge. I learned a lot, I was ready to listen, and indeed, more than one teacher magically appeared.

In later chapters I'll discuss each type of investment I learned about, where we got started, how they were prioritized, and the logical progression that made sense to us. In addition, my natural inclination was to become the modern day Paul Revere, only my message is "Inflation is coming, inflation is coming!" But I didn't have enough patience. Much like it was with Glen Kirsch and me, all I seem to have done with many of our friends and family is overwhelm and frustrate them. What I have finally learned is to take it slow, educate them on the big picture, then take baby steps. It is much easier to drink from a slow-running fountain than from a fire hose.

Chapter 3

JUST WHAT, EXACTLY, IS THE PROBLEM?

I was overwhelmed after my initial discussion with Glen Kirsch. Then another concern became rather apparent. Not only Glen, but also the other folks I looked to for help, were correct in their assessment that indeed it was quite possible that our country could be headed into another period of Jimmy Carter type inflation or possibly worse. What about our family and friends? They're going to be affected too. For the younger ones who are still working, as long as they continue they will survive, just as those of us who lived through the Carter era did. The Carter era certainly had inflation, but nothing near the hyperinflation that our country could be faced with this time.

Most of my peers are seniors, living on fixed incomes, some with portfolio earnings supplementing their Social Security, many living in the North in the summer and the South in the winter. They dine out regularly and play golf whenever they want. For most, their life would seem like the traditional American dream, hopefully being blessed with good health for a few more years and enjoying a casual lifestyle.

NOT BEING HEARD

My first encounter after speaking with Glen was with a group of really good guys who meet every other Tuesday morning for breakfast. We call ourselves "the Romeo Club" (Retired Old Men Eating Out). Every time a politician sets up a special committee to study this or that issue, we like to joke that they should give us the problem and more than likely we could solve it before our second cup of coffee. We are quite confident that there are thousands of groups like ours across the country, and the government would really save a lot of time and money by seeking them out, because they would come up with better solutions for a lot less money and in a fraction of the time it takes a government committee to get to its final report.

During the summer of 2009, members of the Romeo Club asked me to put on a little presentation for them. They have an investment group where everyone puts in $50/month and meets to discuss potential investments. I use the phrase "investment club" somewhat loosely; it's just as much a social club. By that time they knew I was investing in foreign currencies, metals, and other less traditional investments, and they wanted to know why, what type, and how I was finding the investments. That was my first attempt at explaining in a more organized fashion what I feared was taking place.

While I was planning my presentation, I happened to receive a newsletter from a brokerage firm with all the nice glossy stuff, and it was outlining various portfolios in the form of pie charts. It started with aggressive, moderate, and on down to conservative portfolios. I looked at it and was shocked. The "conservative" portfolio was all in US dollars, mostly fixed income with a lot in government bonds. No gold nor silver was recommended.

Just What, Exactly, is the Problem?

I made a copy of that chart and used it to start my presentation. My message was, "If this is what your broker is telling you, I suggest you run for the hills." I then showed some the charts about government spending, with curves starting to point skyward and tying them to the idea that the spending will eventually cause Jimmy Carter-type inflation. I stated that at one time a good investor was one who could beat the S&P 500, but now I felt a good investor was someone who could garner after-tax returns that kept ahead of inflation. From there I outlined some of the investments my wife and I had moved into, including moving a good bit of my Roth IRA offshore legally (and I emphasized "legally").

I was speaking to a group of some pretty nice guys; they had good questions and were interested. But I also realized that for them the meeting was "informational" at best. It was not likely that any of them were going to be really changing their investment philosophy.

Not two weeks later the Sovereign Society sent out a newsletter showing the identical graph and said, "If this is what your broker is telling you to do, we suggest you get another broker." While I felt somewhat vindicated and actually distributed the article at the next Romeo breakfast, not much really changed. I was baffled. How come the threat that I felt I understood so clearly was not being seen by others?

I later learned that some went back to their "guy," either a money manager or a stockbroker, whom they had known for years and basically they were told, "No big deal, we have 10% of your portfolio in Treasury Inflation Protected Securities (TIPS) or

similar type investments, to hedge against inflation." None had anything in gold or silver, as I recall. There was a huge gap between what I was reading in *The Casey Report* and what I was learning from our money manager in Europe who was looking after my Roth IRA, versus what the US folks were telling their clients.

As this is being written, we are well into the third year of having to self-manage part of our investment portfolio. We now have the advantage of three years of hindsight.

UP AND DOWN AND HESITATE

During the summer of 2011, we did an analysis of our total investment portfolio's performance year to date, and we were up 20% for the year in real numbers. Then in a short time, gold and silver prices dropped like a rock, which of course brought down our other metal investments right along with them. We went from up 20% to down 10%, a swing that scared the daylights out of us. It certainly caused us to question the entire concept of preparing for hyperinflation. Maybe we weren't on the right track.

In one of the Casey newsletters, David Galland had suggested that the summer might be a little bumpy, and that one might consider taking some profits and having some cash on hand. Fortunately, we had done that. But as prices headed lower and lower, we wished we had done it a whole lot more.

We wondered whether we should pull off our road, slip into a rest stop, take a breather from our journey, and once again try

to look at the big picture. Most every newsletter we received was screaming "Don't panic," and insisting that the fundamentals hadn't changed. They showed that gold and silver had gone through much bigger swings before and that we were still in a bull market. "Just hang on" was the message. That's when I decided to spend the money to fly to Phoenix and attend the Casey/Sprott *When Money Dies* conference. My assumption was I would be among like-minded people, with similar concerns, and would hear a roster of speakers who were most qualified to address the issues. My assumption turned out to be correct.

We also came to an important conclusion. Originally our government had a $500-billion budget deficit, followed by a $500-billion TARP bill, which started our concern about inflation. Then we had two Quantitative Easing (QE I & QE II) programs that were well over a trillion dollars. Our budget deficits were triple what they were when we first began to realize that Jimmy Carter-type inflation was a real possibility. We were reading that the government might run into trouble auctioning Treasury bills (which it needs to do almost every week). I had to explain to my wife that it meant that others were looking at the US government, realized it had become a credit risk, and were no longer willing to lend to it as easily as they had in the past.

DOLLAR SPLIT

What was really keeping the T-bill auctions going was this: If the Treasury needed to raise $100 billion at an auction, foreign governments and other investors might only buy $60 billion worth. Rather than up the interest rates to attract more foreign investors – which would mean even bigger budget deficits for the government – certain "private dealers" would buy up the remainder and in turn sell it to the Federal Reserve three days later. In essence, that meant whatever money folks wouldn't lend the US government, the Federal Reserve would create out of thin air with a bookkeeping entry in their computer. Now, I might not remember much from taking economics courses, but I do remember that inflation comes from government deficits accompanied by an increase in the currency supply. Each additional dollar printed or created by the Federal Reserve devalues the currency already in circulation.

If you own shares in a company and they have a two-for-one stock split, the value of the company doesn't change. Instead, you own twice as many shares, but each share is worth half what it was before the split. Each share is devalued. When I saw the FDIC graph showing that total bank deposits had gone from $4 trillion in the year 2000 to $10 trillion in 2010, my first reaction was, "Isn't this really the same thing? Isn't it a two-and-a-half-for-one "stock split" in the dollar?"

As mentioned earlier, it wasn't until I went to the Casey/ Sprott conference that I realized I had totally underestimated the problems looming on the horizon for our country.

The other conclusion we came to was that since 2008, the fundamentals hadn't changed. If anything they had gotten much, much worse. Budget deficits had tripled, cash supply had jumped radically, and there were calls for another huge Quantitative Easing by the Federal Reserve (although they were going to call it something else because the public had soured on that term and were tired of bailing out banks). Welfare, the volume of food stamps, and the money paid out in unemployment compensation would have been unthinkable just a few short years ago.

After the conference we sat down and discussed our position. We concluded that, despite some scary short-term losses, we were going to stay the course. None of the reasons behind making our investments had really changed, in our opinion. The need to protect ourselves from inflation was clearer to us than it was in 2008. Bottom line is we pulled out from our temporary rest area and continued on our journey, more confident than ever that we were on the right path... just hoping that sooner rather than later gold and silver prices would resume their upward trend.

That experience leads me to our second suggestion: **Do not even begin to think about investments for protecting yourself against inflation until you feel you really understand the potential problem on the horizon and understand it both financially and emotionally.**

THE TASTE OF HYPERINFLATION

Included in the conference in Phoenix was a panel of gentlemen from Argentina, Yugoslavia, and Zimbabwe. They discussed their personal experiences with hyperinflation. They described it as living through a collapse, after which they emerged to start again. In each case, the ordeal took around 36 months. For me personally, their stories were the highlight of the conference. Here's why.

I suspect, like a lot of folks, if you were to ask me about inflation, particularly hyperinflation, I would have said something like, "It is bad; your dollar is worth less." Then I might have remembered the lessons from school about the Weimar Republic, where folks got paid at noon and took their money in a wheelbarrow and raced to buy a loaf of bread.

Those of us who lived as adults in the Jimmy Carter inflation era can remember having to wait in line for a couple of hours to buy five gallons of gas. Most of us were working 60 to 80 hours a week to make our house and car payments and put food on the table for our families. I vaguely remember that we wanted to get a bigger home and decided to put it off because mortgage rates were something like 18%. At best I would describe that time as a major inconvenience. The truth is I can hear the word "hyperinflation," but nothing in my life experiences makes me able to truly understand it, much less be able to relate to it.

Each one of the speakers showed photos of the 50-million-dollar bills and the trillion-dollar bills that were being circulated by their governments at the time. One speaker mentioned that at the peak one of the giant bills was worth about ten US dollars. Each showed his inflation graphs with a trendline slowing rising, then going straight up as one said his country's inflation rate was 200,000 percent, while another speaker said that his country went to something like 200 million percent. Now how the heck can anyone in America relate to that? Then the gentleman from Yugoslavia put up a slide following his graph in big, bold, red letters that said, **"On average prices doubled every 1.4 days"** – and the audience gasped!

It was not until I returned home and tried to describe to some folks what life would be like with prices doubling every 1.4 days that the magnitude of the situation became clear to me.

My next suggestion is this: **When you see these types of graphs or charts, try to break the information down into terms you can personally relate to.** Earlier I mentioned that one needed to understand the problem both financially and emotionally. I can assure you that once you figure out what it means financially, the emotional understanding will quickly follow.

Let me give you an example. Friends came to my wife and me for advice. In round numbers, they had a $100,000 CD mature, and they were uncomfortable rolling it over for five years at less than 2% interest. They saw the huge increases in government spending, spending money it doesn't have, and they sensed that such a thing couldn't go on forever. To use their terms, they felt something was "just not right."

My first attempt at explaining hyperinflation was to use the information about prices doubling every 1.4 days. I said if gas is $2 a gallon, in a couple of days it will be $4, then $8, then $16. I stopped at that point because for all of us it was unthinkable; we could not relate to gas selling for $16 a gallon. Based on our life experiences, it was too much of a stretch.

Then it dawned on me – let's try it the other way. I said, "Suppose you decide to roll over your CD for five years and hyperinflation hits during that period. In a period of 1.4 days the buying power of that CD drops to $50,000, then another couple of days, it drops to $25,000, then to $12,500." At that point, I was interrupted by our friend blurting out something to the effect of, "In less than a month your entire life savings would be worthless!"

I will readily admit that is when I also *personally* realized what hyperinflation could really mean to our family, and what the conference speakers meant when they said many senior citizens were totally wiped out. The now much-too-familiar knot in my stomach immediately tightened as the *emotional* impact of that statement hit home.

Being gluttons for emotional punishment, we decided to take a $100,000 CD and see how long it would take for it to be worth less than $1.00 in buying power, applying the 1.4 days experience that happened in Yugoslavia. In less than a month, in just 25 days, the buying power of a $100,000 CD would be reduced to $0.76.

In other words, at the beginning of the month your money would likely buy four Toyota Camrys. Less than a month later, that money wouldn't buy a Hershey's bar. Would there be anything you could buy for 76 cents? There was a reason I chose the Hershey's bar as an example. One of our friends asked, "What would you really do?" My wife blurted out, with a grin on her face, "I'd head for the chocolate!" I pointed out to her it had better be a small bar, because she couldn't afford the big one anymore.

The next question was, "Do you think that can really happen?"

HOMEWORK FOR SURVIVAL

I explained to our friends that just last week I read an article
about the Weimar Republic, what happened leading up to
the hyperinflation, and the results, supported by many charts
and graphs. No need to read the whole article – the summary
paragraph said it all. Just before hyperinflation started, it took
2.4 German marks to buy a loaf of bread. When inflation was at
its peak it took **2.4 trillion** German marks to buy the same loaf
of bread; the government had in effect devalued the mark one
trillion times. We shrugged our shoulders and concluded that
the only difference between a trillion percent inflation and 200
thousand percent inflation is that it takes just a few more days
before your life savings are gone. For those who are retired, I
would add "gone forever."

As an aside, how lucky I was to have read that article just a few
days before. Our friends are under the illusion I'm smart; in fact
I'm just a few miles farther down the road than they are.

It was at that point that I wrote David Galland, as I mentioned
at the beginning of this book. My contention was that the pundits
need to find better ways to relate to their readers than just
graphs, charts, and conclusions. The situation needs to be broken
down into terms that the average person can understand and
relate to. You read David's response: "Dennis, you like to write,
so have at it!"

One more suggestion, and we can move on. In showing our
friends what we were doing, I printed out several newsletters
for them to read, a stack nearly half an inch high. I was asked,

Just What, Exactly, is the Problem?

"Do you really read all this stuff?" I hesitated before I answered, because I felt there was more to the question than they realized.

I asked them how many hours per week both husband and wife had toiled for the 45+ years they worked to accumulate their life savings. They looked at each other and concluded around 65 hours per week. Then I asked, "If you worked so hard to accumulate your life savings, is it worth an hour a day to read and learn what's needed to protect the money you are counting on?" The answer is a no-brainer as soon as you think about the question. My next suggestion is easy: **Commit yourself to spend the time to educate yourself on investments and what is going on in the world.**

My personal experience is that staying on top of things is not as difficult as it may appear at first. When the daily reports come in during the morning, I print them out and read them with the morning paper. Anything that arrives in the afternoon goes on my reading table and gets read before bedtime. As a senior with trifocal glasses, I much prefer to read from paper than from the computer, so that's what works for me. One more tip: With the click of a mouse, you can have the printer print on both sides of the page, which cuts the paper cost in half.

By now you likely are motivated. Remember, motivation by itself energizes incompetence. Reading good newsletters and reports can boost your competence in a big way in a short time. I don't know what it is about seniors, but once they retire they think their investments will manage themselves. As I mentioned to a friend of mine, "You'd better take the time to read and learn, because it's your investment capital that is allowing you to play golf three days a week. Lose your money, lose your golf, plain and simple."

37

THE GRAVITY OF THE PROBLEM

Let's quickly summarize where we are. One needs to understand the gravity of the potential problem. I cannot imagine that anyone who understands what waits on the horizon wouldn't be motivated to rethink their entire investment philosophy and then move most of their capital into investments that will offer the most protection. At the same time, I want to remind folks of the first lesson I learned: Get a grip! Don't let emotions and fears keep you from thinking everything through before you act.

I want to reiterate a suggestion I made earlier: **Do not even begin to think about investments to deal with protecting yourself against inflation until you feel you really understand the potential problem on the horizon both financially and emotionally.**

Readers may wish to take a minute and look at a simple little formula I developed as a check to see how you are currently doing investment-wise in protecting yourself against the effects of inflation. Are you ahead of the game or losing ground?

1. Go to www.shadowstats.com and you will see the current inflation rate calculated the way the government used to do it, before it passed the law indexing Social Security checks to inflation. Now the government uses a different method; among other things, it ignores the effects of price increases for food and fuel. Perhaps they think most Americans don't eat or drive to the store. I will assume for the sake of an example that Shadowstats' accurate measure of inflation puts it at 7%.

2. Go to your most recent full-year investment numbers and calculate your return (our Quicken program calculates it for us). For the sake of illustration, assume you are up 10%.

3. You must then take into consideration the income taxes you pay. I suggest just using the marginal tax rate you paid last year. For my example, I'm using 30%. Now, the big-time accountants are going to get all twisted into a knot pointing out that it depends on when you take your profits; and some profits can be taxed at regular rates while others are taxed as long-term capital gains. To them I say, "Chill out!" If you start with all the complications and exceptions, you no longer have a "simple little formula," or what is commonly known as a "rule of thumb."

4. Then calculate the amount of pre-tax return you would need to earn to keep up with inflation. In other words, what is our true, after-tax return on our investment portfolio? In the case of our example, a 10% return before taxes which would net 7% after taxes. So a 10% return is what you would need to keep up with inflation.

Here comes the hard part. Again taking a nice round number, assume you started the year with $1 million invested, and after taxes you ended up with a 7% return. That means you have an additional $70,000 in your investment account. You might feel richer, but are you really? In truth, the money in your investment account will buy no more than it did at the beginning of the year. During inflation, that's not such a bad result; at least you stayed even.

Just What, Exactly, is the Problem?

For what it is worth, inflation in the Carter era was as high as 14.6%. Someone in the 30% tax bracket had to earn a 20.9% return on their invested capital before taxes *just to stay even!* It is easy to see why Bud Conrad and others talk about how inflation erodes citizens' buying power. Those with jobs will see their wages rise, which helps to make up for higher prices at the store. Senior citizens with fixed incomes, on the other hand, have a much greater challenge with Carter-era inflation rates. But hyperinflation? I wouldn't know where to start. To keep up, your returns would have to be astronomical. I guess that is why so many folks are suggesting gold and silver.

As we have all learned in life, before you can put together a plan, you must have a clear goal. In our case, the goal is to take our life savings and invest it prudently in assets that will protect us from the ravages of hyperinflation. The days of our government's excesses, spending more than they take in, are coming to an end. At one time, lending money to the US government was the safest thing you could do. T-bills were as "good as gold." Now many countries are shedding their US Treasury holdings out of fear. They've stopped lending to our government. Our credit rating as a nation has been downgraded. Many countries and central banks have over the last few years added many tons of gold and silver to their vaults, and they are stepping up the pace of accumulation.

Our goal is now clear – to both stay ahead of inflation and to supplement our Social Security and other retirement income. We have taken more than one deep breath, and now it is time for a plan. We will next discuss an overall investment philosophy, then review the kind and types of investment we felt most comfortable with. The journey continues...

Chapter 4

IT IS TIME TO GET STARTED

Assuming you have a sense of the problems that lie ahead for our economy, let's start looking at a realistic course of action for protecting your life savings.

At one time in my career I wrote textbook material on "problem solving" and taught a course on the subject. It was fun, because I would have the students use their real business problems as topics for discussion, so they were really engaged. I want to borrow some of the phrases we used at the time.

One of the most difficult challenges for the students was to identify the real problem and understand it separately from its symptoms. For example, imagine I have a terrible pain low on the side of my abdomen. Is the problem a pain in my side, or could the pain be a symptom of something else, like appendicitis? To further complicate things, sometimes what we found was a tangle of interrelated problems. When that happened, we called the whole thing a "mess." The best way to solve a mess is to break it down into its smallest parts. That leaves you with manageable chunks you can deal with individually.

From this point forward, we are going to break each problem down into smaller issues and deal with them one by one.

A lot of seniors who have accumulated wealth were either self-employed or worked in a job that required a whole lot more than a 40-hour workweek. We called them "rainmakers," because they had the ability to make a lot of money from their efforts.

Because these folks were so busy, many had accountants, brokers, money managers, or advisors to help them. They delegated some or perhaps all the responsibility for looking after their money. To save time, I am going to use "advisor" as a catch-all, meaning any of the four types just listed.

THE ADVISOR DECISION

For most, the first decision is: **Do you continue to delegate to your advisor or do you become a Do-It-Yourself (DIY) investor?** As I mentioned earlier, when the "nice lady" (who really was a help) retired, we chose the DIY route and put all our money in CDs. Maintaining a CD ladder was not that difficult for us.

A CD ladder is a pretty easy thing to understand. We had our entire life savings in CDs, so we wanted each CD to be small enough to be totally insured by the FDIC. At the time, that meant nothing larger than $100,000. As a result, we had money at several in banks scattered around the country.

With a CD ladder, you always keep part of your money in long-term CDs (for higher yield) and still have enough deposits maturing every year to handle any emergency. You begin by deciding how much you want to have maturing every year. To keep the math simple, I'll assume it's $100,000 per year, meaning you would select maturity dates so that $100,000 worth will mature during the course of every year. Next, you take the total amount you have to invest; say it's $500,000. You would then buy CDs with different maturity dates, so that the $100,000 matures in years 1, 2, 3, 4, and 5. Each year, as a CD pays off, you replace it with a new one with a five-year maturity. The idea is to keep them spaced out, particularly because in those days, the longer the term of the CD, the higher the yield.

There were a couple of times when I found CDs with interest rates as high as 7% going out 7-9 years; I grabbed them and then readjusted the ladder as the next few CDs matured. At the time, CDs worked well for us. But in the years just ahead, a CD ladder could turn out to be a ladder to the poorhouse.

Our next recommendation is this: **Do not assume your advisor – who may well have looked after your money for years – is always the best option.** Now is a good time to re-evaluate their skills and your relationship.

At the time we moved everything into CDs, I did not have a good feeling about fee-based money managers. My attitude was based on a single experience, and it wasn't even my own. One of my dear friends was a successful member of the medical profession, a true "rainmaker." He sold some of his investment property and found he had $3 million cash on hand. He said he had a problem in that he didn't have time to really manage his money. Most of us would be more than happy to trade places with him and try to figure it out.

He decided to hire a money manager, and he showed me all the glossy brochures, full of disclaimers. The stated goal was to be conservative but try to beat the S&P 500; the philosophy was steady, consistent, long-term growth. He and his wife met the manager for dinner; they had a two-hour meeting. After the meeting, my friend put his money under the manager's control. The contract was for one year and was renewable annually.

At the end of the year, he could not get his money back fast enough. He told me that if he could, he would have fired the manager earlier in the year. I asked him if he had lost any of his money and he said, "No, not really."

He went on to explain that once the manager took over, he barely heard from him except for the reports he received by mail. He would place a phone call and it might take 2-3 days to get a return call, and many times he felt like he was imposing on the manager's time. What he discovered was that this particular individual worked for a large firm and personally looked after several clients; the total combined portfolios of the entire group was well over a billion dollars. Many individual accounts were over $25 million. Now, $3 million may seem like a virtual fortune to most of us, but compared to the manager's big accounts, my friend was a small-potatoes customer. He sarcastically mentioned that he sometimes wondered if it was the money manager' s secretary who really looked after his money.

We concluded that he really hadn't done a good job of screening potential managers but also that the money manager had set up unrealistic expectations as to the level of service he was willing to give.

GRADING YOUR ADVISOR

If you are currently using a money manager or other advisor, how would you determine if he is doing the job of protecting you from what the future may hold? One of the difficult issues is this: you need to set aside friendship and personality. Evaluating an advisor's performance is nothing personal. Senior citizens in particular do not get a do-over. For most, the money in their brokerage account plus their homes and autos represents the savings accumulated over their lifetime. If your advisor does a poor job and loses a big chunk of your money, the advisor loses a client, but you lose your security. **Quite simply, you must test the advisor's performance by reviewing your portfolio objectively on a regular basis in light of what is going on in the world both economically and politically.**

Don't over-rely on the advisor's track record. Remember the saying on most every mutual fund prospectus ever printed: "Past performance does not guarantee future results."

The most basic question when you review your portfolio is not to look at the individual investments and whether they are up or down, but rather, will this group of investments grow, generate enough income and protect my family going into the future? Today we are concerned about hyperinflation, and certainly the effects of that can be devastating for an investor.

On the other hand, things can change rather quickly. In the Jimmy Carter era, we experienced inflation in the range of 20%. Then the Federal Reserve signaled it was going all out to bring down inflation and began raising interest rates to pull money out of the economy. One must realize that it hadn't solved the problem of high inflation; however, the signal to the market caused the prices of metals and metal stocks to come crashing down.

Today we are looking at investments with the goal of protecting against high inflation. But that could quickly change, so you might evaluate your portfolio – and your advisor – to determine if the portfolio would survive with rapidly deteriorating metals prices. Also, the federal government could radically change the tax structure. Are you protected against a potentially huge tax burden?

More than once, a Casey newsletter has observed that generals always prepare to fight the last war. Unfortunately, many investment advisors prepare their clients to deal with the last crisis, not the one just ahead.

If you're not satisfied with what your advisor is doing, you don't necessarily need to fire him on the spot. A more prudent approach would be to bring him some information, voice your concerns, and ask for his plan to address them. Then you have a choice to make. One way or another, you'll know that your investment mix must be changed in light of changes in the world around us. But don't stop listening. If your existing advisor doesn't seem to accept your vision of where inflation is taking us, hear what he has to say. After that, if you still feel you are right, then it is time to consider alternatives. Your investment mix needs to be ready when market events occur for you to profit; not acting in a timely manner can be costly.

CASE STUDY

One of our Romeo friends who now understands the risks we discussed earlier asked me this question: "My guy who I have worked with for years just does not 'get it,' no matter how I try to explain it to him. Not quite sure yet what I should do. Any suggestions?"

We looked at the potential options and came up with these:

1. Fire the advisor and look for a new one.

2. Fire the advisor and take over the job himself.

3. Do somewhat of a hybrid – keep the advisor but take a more active role in directing his own investments.

I mentioned option #3 because I knew of a case where it was done. I'll address this possibility first, because it is the least complicated.

My friend had really studied the material I sent him and understood that indeed there are huge potential problems on the horizon. He had a clever idea of diversification that I had never thought of. He personally had never considered a professional, fee-based money manager. Instead he split his investment money up between two stockbrokers at different firms. He simply stated that two heads are better than one. He felt that his idea worked for him, as he shared cases where each broker found different investment opportunities that had been profitable.

On the other hand, when he looked at where most of his

money was invested, he became concerned. It was, as he termed it, "traditional US companies," all denominated in US dollars, and nothing in metals or metal stocks. Neither broker really had him ready for high inflation. When he told me his "guy" didn't get it, he really meant neither of his "guys" seemed to understand what he was talking about.

He devised what I thought was a clever plan. He selected one of the investment newsletters he read that was full of graphs and charts showing why investors had better be protecting themselves from the inevitable inflation that's coming. I like Doug Casey's remark, "Just because something is inevitable does not mean it is imminent." The author of the newsletter did not predict a time frame, but he did try to create a sense of urgency.

My friend made an appointment to visit each broker and brought a copy of the newsletter with him. He told each broker two things. 1. He was very concerned about what the author had to say and felt steps needed to be taken with his money to address the inflation issue; and 2. He had another account of similar size with another broker. He was asking each broker to put together a plan. He would look them both over, choose what he felt was the best one, and move all his money into one account. His thought was that by explaining the problem to both of them and setting up an incentive, they each would spend time on it and get creative and offer some good ideas.

About a month later I asked him how it worked out. He reported he was really unhappy with both plans: neither of his guys really seemed to understand. One broker had taken the time and offered some good ideas on selling some of his positions and buying some gold and silver stocks. The other suggested selling a couple of stocks with a loss and buying Treasury Inflation Protected Securities (TIPS). With the first broker's plan, about 20% of the portfolio would have been in investments that would help combat inflation. With the second broker, less than 15% of his invested capital would end up in TIPS.

My next question was, "Wow! What are you going to do?" He concluded that he had a better relationship with broker #1, who was also the younger of the two. So he closed out the account with the #2 broker and moved his money over. He told broker #1 he would like to start meeting with him regularly, and they would decide together how to allocate his life savings. In essence, he chose the option of trying to educate his advisor.

In summary, there are several things to consider:

1. In dealing with an investment advisor, you must be honest with yourself. Try to separate friendship from results.

2. Ask yourself whether your current advisor really understands and has a vision of what's coming that is similar to yours. A good way to find out is to ask him what he's already done for some of his other clients who take inflation risk seriously.

3. Do you have the time to be a DIY investor? If it's not realistic to think that you do, then you have two challenges. The first is to find someone who can do the job. The second is to educate yourself, in effect, on how to manage your advisor. By that I mean find ways to quickly understand where you are and recognize whether you are still on track.

It is Time to Get Started

The next step is for us to discuss in detail how one might go about finding a good advisor.

In case you decide to go the DIY route, I'll outline some of the struggles we went through before we learned to build an overall strategy, and then give some tips for filtering through what will be hundreds, if not thousands of potential investments. We will discuss how and why we chose to take a pass on some and act on others.

Chapter 5

THERE ARE LOTS OF FOLKS WHO WANT TO HELP

In 1990, my age clock ticked past the half-century mark. Many of my peers used to casually discuss their "portfolios." I would listen and even try to sound intelligent; however, I had a difficult time relating.

I had divorced in my mid 40s and remarried a few years later, and that meant starting over financially. No regrets; it was the right decision for me and for my ex-wife, and I would do the same thing again. It's just the way it was. It happened at the same time that the Internet bubble was starting to inflate, so the stock market and investments were a common topic of conversation.

The reason I had a tough time relating was simple. My finances consisted of a home with a mortgage, two cars (one paid for), a bit of money in the bank, and a brokerage account with a balance that we could probably have lived on for maybe six months. Sad to say, it also included a small boat on which I owed a good deal more than the boat was worth. I don't ever recall discussing my "portfolio" with my friends as much as we would discuss individual investments.

At the same time, I had turned the corner toward my peak earning years. My children were out of college; one was married with two children. I had just broken away from a group of partners I had worked with for many years, and I'd gone into business for myself. When the decision was made to go into my own business, I told one close friend, "If I can make it go, just maybe I can catch up with my peers. If not, likely my wife and I will retire in a double-wide."

Forty weeks per year traveling and 80+ hour work-weeks were the norm for quite some time, working elbow to elbow with my new bride. Luckily we turned the corner and saw our income rise above our expenses. Instead of spending like we might have done in our 30s, we knew we had to start really trying to save money, because we were getting older and there was no way we could keep up the pace for another decade or more. We needed to accumulate money that could be invested and continue to compound in our brokerage account. We longed for the day when investment income would match our current earnings.

As we began to prosper, we found well-intended friends trying to guide us to folks with titles like fee-based "money manager," "estate planner," "stockbroker," and even a "certified public accountant" (CPA), who promoted himself as qualified to look at our net worth and able to offer guidance.

THE RIGHT HELP

On the top of this page it says "There are lots of folks who want to help;" let me now finish the sentence: "and that can sometimes be a real problem." How do you find a good one? How can you find one you can really trust? What should you look for? How would you go about interviewing the candidates? And the first big hurdle for us: "Do we really need a manager, or are we kidding ourselves?"

At the time we had become close friends with the "nice lady," who we will now refer to as our "broker friend." (She has now been retired well over a decade, and we are still in touch with one another.) The amount of time she spent educating us was not in proportion to the size of our account. She also looked after Grandma's account, but we gradually eased into CDs which we purchased through her firm. I know she was paid commissions on stock trades. That was easy to see, because there was a commission charge on every trade confirmation. I knew she was good and was well paid, because she had been recruited by another firm and given a nice bonus to join them, with the hope she would bring all her accounts with her. Grandma and I followed right along; she was really someone we could totally trust and still do today.

Grandma spent the last several years of her life in an assisted living facility, and our broker friend would look after her a bit. We had moved to Tampa, so we were a couple of hours away. Many times she lamented to us that a good client, one she served for 20 years or more, had passed away. She became almost a godmother to many a widow in her 80s and looked after them and their portfolios. To us she passed along what I later realized was the most important criterion one should consider in attempting to find an advisor: ***she truly cared about her clients and their well-being***.

She got into trouble with her firm because she wasn't pushing some of the products they were trying to sell. They called her into her boss' office, and she stood her ground. She called me after the meeting, and we actually met for lunch. She was most emphatic that she would sell their products when she thought they were good for her clients. She would not be pushed into supporting what she considered some of their inferior products. How blessed we had been a few years earlier that when our old broker left, the office divided up his client base, and we ended up on her list to call. We found her, or she found us, by the luck of the draw.

As she was getting ready to retire, I asked her how we would ever find another one as good as her. I had been to her office and saw way too many hotshot young men in their late 30s or early 40s wearing expensive suits and driving their hot Porsches, and I knew they were not where I wanted to end up. I trained thousands of salespeople in my career, and I used to try to tell the younger ones in particular, "Don't get hoodwinked into thinking the job is easy." I said, "It's easy to sell when times are good; it's when times are tough that you test the mettle of your sales force." As I looked at those young stockbrokers, I would think to myself, *They appear to think they are pretty hot stuff. I wonder how many will survive the next time stocks go into a long bear market?*

In November 2011 I saw a paragraph in the *Casey Daily Dispatch* that really makes the point. Here is what it said:

"For those who haven't heard of Bill Miller, he's a legend in the mutual-fund world. He beat the S&P 500 for 15 years in a row, until being severely derailed by the 2008 crash. However, his fund has underperformed the market for the past four out of five years. As a result, Miller is retiring from his once-famous fund. So, what happened? Essentially, Bill is an expert at bull markets. When the sun is shining, one couldn't be in a better fund. However, he apparently has absolutely zero grasp of markets in a slump. He kept making bullish bets expecting yet more sunshine and roses ahead. Unfortunately for him, this optimistic scenario never materialized. The crisis claims another optimist."

As I read that, I wondered how many managers of company pension funds, brokers looking after their clients' 401k accounts, and individuals following the shining star who had beat the S&P 500 for 15 years in a row (which is quite an accomplishment) had decided that putting money in the fund was a safe, conservative choice. How much money did they need to lose before they realized after 2008 that the money should be invested elsewhere?

I wondered if the manager's real mistake was failing to recognize the trend. Certainly the bulk of the newsletters and articles I subscribe to have had nothing but realistic (and gloomy) predictions for the economy, particularly when it comes to real estate. When one looks at the backlog of foreclosed and soon-to-be foreclosed residential and commercial properties and couples it with the real unemployment numbers, it is easy to agree with many of the pundits who suggest that recovery is going to take a good long time.

Just because your advisor may have done well for you in the past is no guarantee. As the prospectus says, "Past performance does not guarantee future results," particularly when there is a significant change in market fundamentals. Some may do well when times are good; others may fare better in tough economic times. Some may do well in times of high inflation, and others may do well at recognizing the impact of major changes in government regulations or tax laws. Regardless, it is **your** life's savings that are at risk, so you need to be sure you are constantly monitoring the situation.

TYPES OF HELPERS

Our broker friend gave me what I considered to be a good education. We discussed various types of advisors. Basically she indicated there were three main groups:

1. Stockbrokers

2. Insurance brokers

3. Fee-based money managers

Each of them would likely have a bunch of initials on his business card indicating a high level of education and licensing. For example, most had CFP, which stands for "certified financial planner." Now I thought that sounded pretty good, until she pointed her finger in the air to interrupt me and began with "however."

The situation she outlined was this. Most all of those who indeed are CFPs are qualified to look at your estate, your age, lifestyle, and all the other parameters they are taught to consider. They will then sit down with you and point out where you may be vulnerable, and they'll be 100% honest.

"Then," she said, "it gets a bit tacky." The stockbroker

recommends solutions, and it is almost always investment products that he happens to sell and his company specializes in.

The insurance broker presents the wonderful investment products his insurance company has to offer that will completely address the issue.

I asked, "Why?" I felt a bit stupid when she said that up to that point they haven't earned a dime, yet they may have invested several hours gathering and analyzing your information. They make their money on the commissions from the products that they sell you after they have done the analysis. She went on to explain that what really happens is this: They have a form for compiling a client's data. The data are fed into their company computer, which digests the information and spits out the company's best products to address the issues.

In a flash, a thought occurred to me. About three months earlier our broker friend had called and asked me some questions. Grandma owned one-third of a farm that had been in the family for almost a century. (She knew about the farm because Grandma would get a small income check each year and we would deposit it in her brokerage account.) She began to query me about the prices of farmland in that particular part of the country. Grandma's sister had passed away, and the farm had to be appraised for her estate. Grandma and her brother were also given a copy of the appraisal. I just gave her the numbers from the appraisal sheet.

She asked me to pull out the last monthly statement for Grandma's account. She then took the total number of acres on the farm, divided by one-third, and came up with a number. Next, she multiplied that by the appraisal price per acre to determine Grandma's equity in the farm. Then she added in the amount from the bottom of Grandma's last monthly statement and came up with a grand total. It was at that point that she began discussing estate taxes and what they could be on an estate the size of Grandma's.

What it boiled down to was that if she had died at that very moment, there was a good chance that the government would want estate taxes in excess of the amount of money in her brokerage account. It was very unlikely that the rest of the family would want to sell the farm, so my wife and her sister would have to make up the balance of her estate taxes out of their pockets. In the end, our broker friend was instrumental in getting a life-insurance policy on Grandma that would cover the estate taxes even though the high premiums reduced the amount in her brokerage account. At the time, I thought it was pretty unusual for a stockbroker to call a client and tell them they need to buy life insurance and right away. I guess we had a genuine, true estate planner without realizing it.

Now I began to understand what she was trying to tell me. If one is going to use an investment advisor, her suggestion was that one is better off with one that is fee-based (their charges are based on a percentage of the total amount of money they look after), because they can pick and choose from various investment products and do the right thing. They are not driven to a particular investment because of a commission or because their company judges their performance by how much of a particular investment product they sell. I thought to myself, "Finding another one like her is like looking for a needle in a haystack." The only manager that I knew we could trust was getting ready to retire.

AFTER FIFTEEN YEARS THE EASY WAY

Those were the factors in our decision to go the DIY route and put all the money in CDs before she retired.

That worked for us for fifteen years. It was in early 2009 that Glen Kirsch urged us to consider a professional, fee-based investment advisor. I must have been a problem for Glen, because I was really opposed to the idea – particularly after my friend told me of his bad experience. On top of that, I had a real bias, feeling it was folks like Donald Trump or Bill Gates – the real financial big boys – who would use a fee-based advisor. I told Glen about my friend's disappointing experience with handing his $3 million over to an advisor whose typical client had $15 million or more. Why would any manager like that want to waste his time on an account like mine?

I had learned over the years that some firms have minimums, and I sure did not want to be embarrassed to find that we are so small we would be turned away. Even worse yet, the last thing we wanted was to have an advisor take us as a client and leave us in the same position our friend found himself in years ago.

Then Glen and I came to an understanding... sort of. He would contact a gentleman named René Schatt, who is a partner in the

firm Weber Hartmann Vrijof & Partners (WHVP). He would ask
René to send me some materials about his firm. I agreed to read
them, make a list of questions I wanted answers to, and then I
would talk directly with Rene. Nothing more was promised, and I
hedged even that commitment. If, after I read the material, I was
really uncomfortable, I could back out of the discussion. Glen
gave me one final piece of advice. He told me to not be shy about
asking questions. If I wanted to know the answer, even if it might
cause some discomfort, ask the question.

Shortly thereafter a large packet arrived. I read it, made a list
of questions, and then set it aside for a while. Then I repeated
the exercise a couple of days later. There were several things
that I was quite impressed with. They did not promise the moon
nor make unrealistic projections or claims; they seemed very
conservative, and I liked that.

On the other hand, there were some things that made me
uncomfortable. There was a section that discussed a client
visiting their offices, and it felt just too polished. During my
business career, I had consulted for some of the absolute titans
of industry. Some folks I worked with were household names. In
several cases I had their home phone numbers. I was certainly
not uncomfortable in that environment. Most of the folks I
worked with at that level were excellent businesspeople, and
they cared little for the fluff; if you were honest and could help
them and their company, nothing else mattered. Once you
were allowed into their inner circle, it was first names, and the
conversation and bantering back and forth might well be no
different than what you'd hear with your bowling team.

What bothered me was this. Long ago I realized whatever success I had in my business and personal life was based on a simple philosophy put forth by my grandmother: be true to yourself and never try to be something you are not. The brochure's picture of the office visit reminded me of an uncomfortable situation I had found myself in some years back. When my wife and I were married, we bought a small home in a country-club community. Included in the maintenance fees was a free dining membership at the club. It probably took us three months before we decided to try eating there; we weren't quite sure we belonged. That probably sounds silly coming from a person who spent many a comfortable night in some of the finest restaurants in the world with top executives of some very large corporations. But the feeling was real.

THE INTERVIEW

I tried to set the tone with René by saying that likely we were both in the process of interviewing each other. If at any point he felt I would not be a good client for his organization, please tell me. The worst thing we could do is start a relationship that wouldn't be good for both of us. Our conversation went something like this:

> I guess the first question I should ask is about minimums. Do you have a minimum size of portfolio for a new client? If you do and I don't meet it, then we are wasting each other's time. (It turned out that we were okay on that point.)

In looking at the brochure, you appear to have a large staff; how big is your firm?

Wow, that's a good size. How many clients do you currently handle?

It sounds like you have quite a good-sized company. How much money in total do you manage for your clients?

I quickly divided the total funds by the number of clients and learned the average portfolio size. As explained earlier, that was an issue that was very important to me. It looked like our account would be okay; we were still in the game.

I then told him about my friend who sent $3 million to an advisor, only to realize that the advisor saw his money as small potatoes.

At that point René elaborated that they have one or two large clients, but most were just folks like me.

Then I asked if he had any questions for me. He started by asking what my expectations would be, and I told him. He then went on to discuss their investment philosophy and wanted to be absolutely sure that my expectations were realistic.

I remember that he surprised me by asking how much I had invested in gold and silver. (The reason he asked will become apparent in the module on determining an overall investment philosophy.) It became clear to me that he did not want to act independently – he would work in tandem with me and consider investments we might have in other accounts. I was glad he raised the issue; it was a question I hadn't thought of, and I realized there were more.

> What type of investments would you normally make for a client my size?

> What is the fee structure?

> What happens if I die or want to cancel?

> What happens when you retire? (I'd already had one broker friend retire on us and wanted to know whether that issue might come up again.)

> You mentioned we would have quarterly conference calls. What is discussed?

I told him something to the effect of, "I can probably read a chart and see that a particular investment went from point A to point B. Are you open for questions on how you chose a particular investment or why you decided to sell?"

After I was satisfied with the company's philosophy and confirmed that an account our size was indeed the market they served, he seemed to be very straightforward, and the details were understood by both sides. I brought up one remaining issue.

I explained to him I was uncomfortable with some of the things I saw in the brochure. While his $10-million clients might be whisked away in a limousine, dressed in a $1,000 suit, and order the most expensive wine on the menu, that's not who I am. I would more than likely arrive in a taxi, wearing a sport coat with no tie, and order a Diet Coke. I said, "I'm not sure I fit the mold of the type of folks you are used to dealing with." While it was meant and taken as a question, I am sure I blurted it out as a statement.

I remember him laughing and reassuring me I was indeed his typical client. Most of the folks they serve were self-employed, hard-working folks who managed to accumulate some money and wanted to be sure they were protected and did not lose it.

At that point a decision had to be made. If you were to go through the same process and not feel comfortable, I would urge you to **trust your instincts** and make no commitments until you are ready.

Since that experience, I have learned there are many good firms serving their clients well and doing just what most folks want – preserving, protecting, and grow the fruits of their life's work.

Your decision about an advisor could easily be one of the most important investment decisions you will ever make. Find a firm where you and your account are the types they cater to. If you have $15-20 million to be managed, you may very well fit right in with the firm my friend fired over a decade ago.

One final tip: It was a much easier decision for my wife and me when we realized we were not going to send all of our money to René. Instead, we agreed upon an amount and sent it to him. It was not until several months later, when we saw and understood what he was doing, that we decided to send more. Some other things to remember are these:

1. Once the decision is made to send part of your money to someone to manage, unless something really changes, don't look back. The decision is made; now the task is to monitor the advisor's performance.

2. I cannot emphasize enough to trust your instincts. In time, if the advisor does his job, a trusting relationship will grow. Likely you will find yourself discussing many things about life and family. If you cannot picture yourself having a good relationship with the person down the road, my suggestion is to look elsewhere.

3. Before sending any money, discuss the procedure for leaving the advisor. After a few months, if for some reason you are not comfortable, a good advisor will understand. Discussing that possibility up front won't be a problem for a good advisor.

4. Once you have a relationship, learn from it. There are many times I will see René invest in something I have never heard of or do not understand. I will discuss it with him and may very well find myself making some changes in the accounts we look after personally.

It was pure luck that we found a nice lady who became our broker and our friend. The chances of having that happen a second time would be slim. Thanks to Glen's insistence, I feel lucky to have found a good advisor on the first try. In effect, Glen – who had many years of experience to guide him – had already culled the market for us.

Chapter 6

TAKING THE PLUNGE!

If you choose the first option I mentioned (fire the advisor and do it yourself), you will be embarking on the same journey my wife and I began when we realized that CDs were no longer the answer. You'll need to speed up your self-education. Personally, I'm not an investment advisor, nor am I qualified to be one. But I was – and am – willing to read and learn.

As stated earlier, one of the reasons behind my writing this little book is the hope that folks can learn from our experiences. Unfortunately, our learning curve cost us a lot of money along the way. What I will be outlining is the process we went through. As I look back, there is much in what we did that I certainly would not recommend to anyone.

I found that many of the free newsletters are valuable and that most of the investment letters worth paying for have a specialty. An issue of a specialty newsletter typically contains buy and sell recommendations, with target prices for one or more "model portfolios." Some paid publications also send out "Alerts," which are time-sensitive reports between regular issues. These hit your inbox when changes in the market call for prompt action on a particular investment.

MY DUMB STRATEGY

At the time, we were seeing our cash balance increase every

month as the CDs kept getting called in, and I felt a great sense of urgency to "do something." Every time a CD would get paid off early, I found myself mentally calculating the annual interest we used to get from it and thinking we just had our income cut by that amount. In retrospect, I feel I was putting way too much pressure on myself.

As I started to read the newsletters, they would give me many stock recommendations. I would read the justification and think to myself, that makes sense. I would normally buy 1,000 shares, because Schwab charged a commission of $8.95 for up to 1,000 shares. Now, how dumb was that? In effect I was making the decision of how many shares to buy based on an $8.95 charge.

After the second month, we had made several stock buys, and the cash balance was down to 10% of the whole portfolio. Along came another issue of a good newsletter with several good suggestions. Each was backed by some darn good reasons, and I realized I no longer had enough money to act on all of them. So now the decision became: What do I sell that was such a great idea last month, so I can buy the new good idea this month? Most of the time I sold the wrong thing and three to four months later would read in the newsletter just how well the stock had performed after I'd sold it.

There's an old saying, "The only thing worse than being lost is being lost and not knowing you are lost." Somewhere in the process, I began to realize I was totally lost. So I started reading more about investment strategies, not just particular investments. Okay, that made sense. What is my current investment strategy? When I figured it out, I didn't like it.

Taking the Plunge!

Buy the investments recommended in newsletters that I receive, based on which letter makes the best case.

Hold the stocks for a short time until I see another recommendation.

When I've forgotten the reason behind buying last month's pick, sell it and buy the new recommendation.

I seriously doubt that the newsletter pundits making the recommendations had that strategy in mind, particularly when you look at their model-portfolio section and see they've held some of their positions for several years. At that point, much as with the exercise program I mentioned earlier, I began to move from the "poor" category and climbed the skill ladder up to "fair." Hey! It was progress.

Before I get into what worked for us, I want to caution you what not to do. Don't try to follow everyone's advice to the letter. For example, in the current edition of the monthly *Casey Report* they have a pie chart suggesting the following:

They begin with 33% in cash, and they break the cash down further into various currencies, so it's not all in US dollars.

The second part is 33% in precious metals (gold and silver).

The last 34% is "other." They break it into a smaller pie chart showing a certain percentage in speculations – some in energy, some international, *etc.* That is what they recommended at the time they published their report.

But I receive other newsletters I respect, and their pie charts have much different allocations. One in particular feels that the best hedge against inflation is to buy TIPS from the federal government, something I personally want no part of.

A BETTER APPROACH

My point is that you will find many suggestions and recommendations, because you want to read and learn from a diversified base. But sometimes that will leave you with the task of sorting through conflicting recommendations. At the *When Money Dies* conference, several speakers were questioned as to how they balance their own portfolios. More than one had a huge percentage in gold and silver, with 80% being in silver. Others had less than half in metals.

It wouldn't take much effort at all to find a pundit somewhere who suggests an allocation pretty close to how your portfolio is invested right now. When I found one who endorsed what I was already doing, my tendency was to say, "I'm cool," and put aside the thought of changing things. Ummmm... in retrospect I don't think that is such a good idea.

Each investor is different. We are different in age, health, portfolio size, family history of longevity, personal risk tolerance, and much more. My suggestion is to learn **why** each pundit is making his suggestions and then decide what allocation is best for you and your family.

I have to confess something here. The fear of the "Don't you dare lose any of mother's money" message I received when I took over for Grandma really overshadowed everything we did. My gosh, I never wanted to look at Grandma or my wife and tell her we lost money here, there, or anywhere. The times we did take a loss were emotionally painful. Perhaps Grandma had a better perspective than I realized at the time. When a woman reaches 85, has been fighting cancer (and managed to live into her early 90s), and knows she has enough money to last until she is 130 according to the investment charts, she might shrug her shoulders and say, "Oh well, no problem" if we lost a couple thousand dollars on a bad investment. While the family was quite pleased that indeed we had done well and not lost Grandma's money, I now realize how much better I could have done while still being very, very conservative. The good news is that no one in the family has or will complain, because realistically none of them wanted the responsibility.

MASLOW'S PYRAMID

I started to read and pay attention to the information about an overall strategy, something more than just trying to pick winners in the stock market. It finally dawned on me that investment strategy was quite comparable to something I had studied many years before. Perhaps some readers might be familiar with Maslow's theory on the "hierarchy of needs." His idea is that the effort to satisfy each human need can begin only when the more basic needs have been addressed.

Taking the Plunge!

Maslow used a pyramid to portray the theory, which makes it fairly easy to grasp. In his view of the world, the most basic of all human needs is survival. It's the first block at the bottom of the pyramid and is the widest. If you wake up hungry each morning and have to hunt for food and water, you had better get on with it or you will starve to death. You can't let anything else get in the way.

Only when you've satisfied your survival needs (perhaps by owning a cow, plot of land, a garden, *etc.*) does the next level on the pyramid come into view. It's called security. As with a squirrel storing nuts or our ancestors canning fruits and vegetables and smoking meat, security really is not much more than "survival for tomorrow."

(In modern-day terms, if one has a job and a large family – as I did at a young age – the first mission is to put food on the table. Many a time in my late 20s I would ask, "How come there is so much month left at the end of the money?" Saving money was the furthest thing from my mind. I was happy if we could keep from going further in debt. I was focused on survival and not yet ready to work for security.)

Maslow continues past survival and security to the psychological needs of man, with the apex being what we used to refer to as "ego" – such as having a school or street named after you. What that top level is for you depends on who you are. For everyone, it is something much more than just survival and security.

I tried thinking about an investment strategy in terms of the Maslow pyramid – Survival, Security, and Something More.

SURVIVAL AND THE CORE

I remember Glen Kirsch telling me about his first job. He was right out of college, working in a hangar on the West coast. His job was to process refugees from Vietnam who were fleeing the country for any number of reasons and coming to America with their family and clothes on their back. He said most of them came with "their little bag of gold." His job was to take that gold and convert it into US dollars so they could begin their new lives in the US. He went on to explain that there were way too many cases when these folks showed up with a suitcase full of Vietnamese currency, and he had to tell them that it was worthless.

Glen then taught me about what he termed "core holdings." I like to describe core holdings as similar to a fire extinguisher; you hope you never need to use it, but it's doggone sure that you need to have it. "Core holdings" was Glen's term for Survival investments.

In the late 1990s Glen recommended that, for core holdings, 5% of your net worth should be in precious metals, with the largest portion being gold. When I spoke to him ten years later, he had had upped his recommendation to 10%.

Personally, I believe an individual needs to decide what is right for himself. It would depend a lot on age, health, family issues, and probably a hundred more variables. For example, if you own a farm and know the family could truly live off the land, you would be much less likely to be as concerned about survival investments than someone living in a luxury condo.

In our case, my wife and I have determined what we want in

our core holdings (the Survival level of our pyramid). We made it a number of coins that can be equally divided among our heirs. No matter what happens to the price of gold and silver, we will not sell the core holdings. It's our "little bag of gold," if you will. We won't touch it except in a dire emergency. We put the coins away and we plan to leave them there.

SECURITY AND THE LONG TERM

Once you determine what your "core holdings" should be, the next level to fill on your pyramid is Security (survival for tomorrow). When discussing this with a friend who's getting close to retirement, he called it "squirreling away as much as you can for retirement." Security investments are what you are going to live on. The Casey Research publication *BIG GOLD* draws a line between long-term investing versus speculation. The former is where you would look for an investment that is fairly safe, provides a good return, and is likely to continue to do so. That's a Security investment.

There are any number of inflation-sturdy investments you could consider for the Security level of your pyramid. These would be more stable, with moderate risk. They include:

- Farmland and artwork, if you have the time and know-how those things require.

- Big gold-mining companies.

- Big oil, like stock in Shell, for example, which pays a dividend.

- Established, mid-level mining stocks.

- Exchange-traded funds (ETFs) that hold gold or silver, such as PHYS (an ETF for gold) or PSLV (an ETF for silver).

- Gold and silver coins and bullion.

- Currencies that have good prospects for avoiding hyperinflation.

SOMETHING MORE AND SPECULATION

On the investment pyramid, Something More means speculation. Many times, one invests in a smaller company where there is a much higher risk in the hope of earning an exceptional return when the company gets discovered by the masses or is taken over by a larger company.

Who wouldn't love to invest early in the next Microsoft or Apple Inc.?

One possibility for inflation-ready speculative investments is the stocks of small companies that explore for gold and silver. There are hundreds of them, and they truly are highly speculative – if finding gold were easy, everyone would be doing it.

An exploration company will drill in the ground where they suspect there may be gold. With enough drill holes, a company can analyze the data and estimate how much gold versus a ton of earth is likely to be in the ground. Then, if the estimate is promising enough, the company will do a business study to determine if mining the gold is economically feasible. Beyond that, it takes a huge financial commitment to build a mine to extract the gold and bring it to market. That's where the successful small exploration company normally will sell out to a giant mining operation.

In essence, the small mining companies are the research arm for the industry. The reason their research is high risk/high reward is that there are many players trying to find gold that can be mined economically; however, only a few are successful. If you have positions in twenty small companies, you would be lucky if two really hit something worth turning into a mine. Boosting your odds is a real science. That's why I use a newsletter specializing in that industry – I don't have the time or expertise to sift through all the possibilities.

Another candidate for the speculative level of your investment pyramid is junior stocks in "emerging technologies." Like the junior mining stocks, they come with a lot of risk, but some have the potential to deliver big profits. Selection is the key.

The speculative level could contain foreign currencies that are likely to appreciate against the dollar. (EverBank has a certificate of deposit that bundles the currencies of emerging countries such as Brazil and China.) It could be any investment that you've decided could go way up or way down in a specified period of time.

Or it might be an option on any of those investments. There are times to buy an option because, for the same money, you can tie up more of the investment. It is a form of leveraging with limited risk. Your risk is the price you paid for the option.

MY PYRAMID

So, the base of the pyramid is your core holdings for Survival. Right above it would be the most conservative investments, solid and safe, for Security. At the top is the smallest portion, being the high-risk or speculative investments, for Something More. Again, the amount at each level of the pyramid should be what you feel comfortable with, and the specific investments for each level can be selected with the guidance of the newsletters and other sources you respect.

You may wonder what percentage of our own investment portfolio is in gold and silver. If I just gave you a percentage, it would really be a disservice. I could say X% in metals. However, looking at all the levels of the pyramid, we may have large and small mining companies, speculative mining investments, and ETFs in gold and silver. If one totaled it all up, our exposure to the ups and downs in the gold and silver markets would be significantly more than X%.

The choice of the investment categories comes first. How much exposure would I want my investment pyramid to have to the metals markets? The second issue is which vehicle is the best? As you put a larger percentage of your investments in a particular category, you need to think about an exit strategy. ***How easy is it for me to liquidate quickly if the fundamentals change in a fundamental way?***

The Investment Pyramid

Speculation
- Junior mining and exploration stocks
- Small- and mid-cap tech stocks
- Junior resource stocks

Moderate Risk
- Some metal stocks
- ETF's, (PSLV, FXA, etc.)
- Stocks

Conservative
- Dividend paying stocks
- Top rated bonds
- Fixed income
- Cash

Core Investment
- Hard assets

Allocation Percentage for Each Category

This is to me a very personal balance. Factors such as age, income, health, and personal risk tolerance are all factors.

In the Survival level of the pyramid we have coins. Some are stored in the US, but most are stored elsewhere. It makes no difference, because we hope we never have to experience the situation of the Vietnamese refugees lining up in front of Glen Kirsch.

Taking the Plunge!

As we move up the pyramid, liquidity becomes very important. For example, if the gold or silver market turns and you have a significant investment in the wrong type of coins, you could become vulnerable. Dealers might be flooded with sellers at the very time you want to get out. Many dealers might stop buying altogether or lowball the price. By the time you liquidate, you could easily lose much of your profit. Contrast that with having an investment in gold and silver stocks or ETFs. They can be liquidated with a click of a mouse any time the exchanges are open.

On the other hand, we found as we got to the top of the pyramid, some of those speculative investments have their own issues. The stocks of small companies may be thinly traded. One investment in particular comes to mind, where the price was $0.48 per share. The newsletter went on about the wonderful discovery the company had made and that it had the potential to be a huge find. I initially decided to buy 20,000 shares, risking $9,600 in total. But when I went to my online trading platform, I saw that about 100,000 shares are traded on a normal day. Had I placed an order for 20,000 shares at one time, it would have been 20% of the usual daily trading volume and the price would have skyrocketed.

To buy the 20,000 shares I wanted without paying too much, I had to slowly feed in buy orders of 1,000 shares at a time, so as to not disrupt the market. It took over a week. The same will hold true when I want to sell. If I put the entire 20,000 shares in on one order, the price will drop like a rock, and that's the price I'll get. I would much prefer the company to be taken over by a buyer that wants to pick up all the shares at a fixed price, so that I can sell all my shares at one time.

YOUR PYRAMID

In summary, my suggestion is for you to build your own pyramid – one that you are comfortable with.

The steps are simple:

1. Take a large sheet of paper and a ruler and draw a pyramid.

2. Draw three levels on the pyramid. From the bottom up, they are:
   Survival – core holdings to keep forever
   Security – conservative and moderate risk
   Something More – speculative investments

3. Go through your entire portfolio and take each investment, one by one, and decide where it belongs on the pyramid.

4. After placing each investment on the pyramid, add up the total investment dollars you have at each level.

5. Then look at the picture. Does it make good sense to you? Do you have the amounts you want at each level? Do you have too high a percentage in speculation and too low a share devoted to core holdings? Or is it, perhaps, the reverse of that?

6. Decide what you feel would be the proper amount for you at each level. Don't be too concerned or too rigid. A few dollars one way or the other is nothing to worry about. But decide.

7. If you feel you are really over- or underweight in a particular
category, then you need to determine what to sell and what
to buy to get to where you want to be. However, don't feel
that "sell" means "sell it all," and "buy" doesn't mean "buy
with both hands." If you have 1,000 shares of something (as
I was prone to do), you may really only need to buy or sell
300 shares to balance things to your comfort level.

Once you have your strategy in place, you then can begin to
look at specific investment opportunities. Our next mission will
be to discuss how to use investment services to our advantage.

The Investment Pyramid

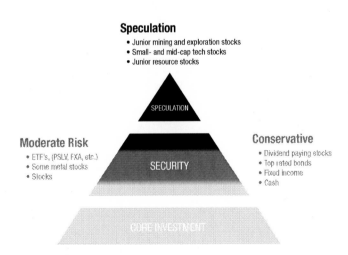

Speculation
- Junior mining and exploration stocks
- Small- and mid-cap tech stocks
- Junior resource stocks

Moderate Risk
- ETF's, (PSLV, FXA, etc.)
- Some metal stocks
- Stocks

Conservative
- Dividend paying stocks
- Top rated bonds
- Fixed income
- Cash

SPECULATION

SECURITY

CORE INVESTMENT

Allocation Percentage for Each Category

This is to me a very personal balance. Factors such as age, income,
health, and personal risk tolerance are all factors.

Chapter 7

USING GOOD RESOURCES

As many folks will tell you, the joys of parenting can be a real challenge, particularly when you are raising teenagers. In those emotional times, when stress levels often run high, the children learn what buttons to push to make the veins stand out in your neck and get you red in the face. For me, that usually happened at a point of exasperation when they had just slam-dunked me in an argument and I knew they were right. It often would be with something like, "In other words, Dad, you are telling us to not do as you do, but rather to do as you say... right?" I can still recall an event like that, trying to make sense with one of my then college-age children. I dropped my voice and said something to the effect of, "Why is it each generation seems to have to learn some things the hard way; why can't they profit from the experience of others?"

When it comes to investing, learning the hard way means learning the expensive way. Let me give you a real-life example.

As I began letting all the newsletters subscriptions lapse, I was selling off investments and putting the money into CDs. But I continued to read the letters that were still coming in, including one by a guru who is well known to investors even today. He suggested buying stock in an electric utility that, to use his terms, "has a rock-solid balance sheet and has increased their dividends each and every year for the last decade." He pointed out that at the stock's current low price, the dividend amounted to an 8% yield. He called it "juicy" and a great investment for grandma who wants a good return. He went on to say that not only could you lock in a terrific dividend return, you would also profit from some stock appreciation.

As luck would have it, we had a fairly substantial CD mature, and the best rate I could find on a new one was around 5%. So we bought the stock and shortly thereafter got a nice quarterly dividend. Then I had another CD mature and bought some more shares.

Less than six months after I read the recommendation, it came to light that the company had some financial problems and cash flow was going to be severely affected. They announced an austerity plan and cut their dividend by 75%, which was followed by a huge drop in the price of the stock. I realized there was little hope of a turnaround for a long time.

Now when one has a stock loss, for tax purposes that loss can offset any gains. And if you don't have any gains to offset, the loss can go against $3,000 of your ordinary income. Any loss you don't use this way to reduce your tax bill can be carried forward to the following year. We ended up with a loss carry forward of around $45,000. I told a friend that I was good for the next 15 years. He laughed, but I didn't think it was so funny.

To me what it represented was a guru's failure to do his homework. He probably had a computer program that sorted for high-yielding stocks. When the company popped up, he did a little research on its history and made the recommendation. Once again we are reminded of the old saying, "If it sounds too good to be true, it probably is."

What are some of the differences between a money manager and people who write newsletters? Whether it is a fee-based money manager or a stock broker, they do the research and then propose the investment. In some cases where they are authorized to do so, they may act on an investment without consulting the client. On the other hand, the stockbroker will likely call and recommend an investment. In either case, it is your money they are investing, you know them, and they have to look you in the eye, win or lose. Winning is more fun for everyone.

For someone who decides to go the Do-It-Yourself route with all or part of his portfolio, the newsletters are a valuable tool. The difference is this: If the newsletter makes a bad call, likely it will lose a subscriber that the writer has never met.

In either case, it is your money that has grown or shrunk, not their own.

TYPES OF NEWSLETTERS

The key to me is picking and relying on the proper sources. Personally, I have newsletters I put into different categories.

One category I call "informational." Some of them make investment recommendations, but I read them just to understand what's going on in the world. Two examples are Ed Steer's *Gold and Silver Daily* and the *Daily Pfennig* written by Chuck Butler of EverBank. They are wonderful summaries, well written and with several references to many other articles of importance. I would personally prefer that as opposed to wading through an expensive *Wall Street Journal*, and they're free.

Another example is the *Currency Capitalist*, which deals in foreign currencies. They really keep me up to date on what is happening in the currency markets, and they do make many recommendations for trades. But I don't need – nor do I intend – to open a forex account. There are other methods for investing in foreign currencies that are better for me. I'll get into them in chapter eight.

A second group of newsletters are the "broad-coverage publications." Examples of the best of them are the *Sovereign Society*, *The Casey Report*, and the quarterly brochure I receive from Charles Schwab, where we have our brokerage accounts. The quarterly from Schwab gives a terrific overview and their model portfolio is much more of what I would refer to as "the big picture." In one of their model portfolios you might well find investments in Shell Oil, Microsoft, an electric utility, a military contractor or two, CDs, some gold and silver, and cash.

The next group is the "specialist" newsletters. Unlike many of the others, these aren't free; you are paying for advice and for the experience of folks who are true experts in a specific area of investments. Under the Casey umbrella, you'll find *BIG GOLD*, *Casey Extraordinary Technology*, and *Casey International Speculator*, to name a few. These provide real, in-depth analysis of the investment candidates they recommend; and in some cases they discuss companies and why they are not yet ready to recommend a purchase.

A LITTLE SKEPTICISM, PLEASE

Now for a bit of my learning curve, kind of the "do-as-I-say" portion of the chapter. Personally, I don't have the skill to sort through thousands of potential investments, nor do I have the willpower to force myself to learn how. Over time I have finally learned that the right newsletters are really valuable in sorting through the suspects to identify the real prospects. Then we, as individual investors, have to cull the list further. We have to look at our entire pyramid, our available cash, and what we may have to use some of that cash for in the near future. It is not fun when you discover that the family car needs to be traded in and you have to sell something to pay for it.

Personally, I feel the specialized investment newsletters, with the right people at the controls, are one of the most valuable tools available. I have had a couple where the individuals at the controls were not as skilled as they needed to be; so you have to select carefully. Let me give you an example.

For a little over a decade during my career, one of my good accounts was Schlumberger. They are a huge company in the oilfield-services business. What they sell helps oil companies find oil, measure how much they've found, and devise the best way to extract it from the earth. The services are very sophisticated and technical and most valuable to their clients.

It wasn't unusual after a training session for Schlumberger to have several of the students ask to trade business cards with me and ask if I might have any interest in looking at some drilling proposals. These folks were on the cutting edge, they knew where the oil was and how to find it, so I said, "Sure, why not?" Soon I began to find my mailbox full of proposals from folks offering me the wonderful opportunity to invest in their drilling project.

Every proposal would include data about the area, other discoveries close by, the seismic test results, you name it. If you're a Casey Research reader, you will know that they really emphasize the "People" aspect of judging an investment. I was surprised to find that in way too many cases, the people who put the deal together and who were offering the fantastic opportunity were the local Holiday Inn owner, State Farm representative, or high-school football coach.

I recall one where I met the student who had put me in touch with the folks who sent the prospectus. He described them in this manner: "Just some good ol' West Texas boys sitting in the bar one night deciding how to get rich in the oil business." Now, that particular prospectus called for a minimum investment of $50,000. It didn't take me long to decide not to even look at them anymore. I didn't understand the technical analysis, and I figured the "good ol' West Texas boys" could just carry on without me and my money.

VALUE OF AN EXPERT FILTER

I have great respect for those who are truly specialists in the segments they write about. In the Casey newsletters, for example, they will give the full background of each senior person in a company – including where they have been before in the mining industry and the successes they have achieved. In some cases, the writer of the report may have known and personally invested with the people in the past. The writer presents the case for considering the investment, and then the reader can make an intelligent decision. I have often wondered how many hundreds if not thousands of "deals" are brought to the Casey analysts for review, and how they are culled to the few that make their short list.

A word of caution here. As I started to read many of the specialized newsletters, it became pretty apparent to me that most of these folks are truly knowledgeable in their particular field. Particularly when it comes to the speculative investments (the narrowest portion on the top of the pyramid), the idea of a spectacular gain is pretty appealing. Some of the recommendations might be stocks priced under $1.00 per share. My natural inclination was to try to buy enough shares that my position would have a lottery-ticket-like power to change my lifestyle.

As an aside, right after my wife and I were married , we bought a lottery ticket in Texas that had six numbers; get them all and you win the big prize, which was $60 million. We had the first five numbers in the string, so we ended up with five of six. You stare at the ticket and hope to somehow magically make that last number on the string change Our prize was $1,500, and it didn't change our life one bit. If anything, it hooks you on the game, and you end up buying more lottery tickets. Now the prizes are huge, but when you read the small print on the back, the odds are generally well over 100 million to one against you.

The speculative newsletters do a good job of reminding you that their recommendations are indeed speculative – maybe big returns, maybe big losses. With the good letters, your odds of winning are certainly better than with the lottery. When a recommendation does hit, the return isn't as astronomical as a winning lottery ticket, but it can be much, much higher than on a conservative investment.

Personally, I feel the reason for a newsletter's success is that the writer reviews hundreds, if not thousands, of opportunities every year. This is particularly true with gold and silver mining, because there are so many little companies. Mining companies know full well what a recommendation from the Casey group can mean for their ability to raise capital, so they seek them out and asked to be reviewed. Go to almost any money conference and you will find rows of booths manned by mining and energy companies with tons of information for potential investors. The stocks discussed in a specialty newsletter are a precious few as compared to the hundreds of possibilities I would have to sort through if I attempted it on my own. To me, that's why a subscription is worth paying for. Not only are you buying a whole lot of research that is done behind the scenes, you are paying for a whole lot more success.

The authors of the newsletters I subscribed to didn't misrepresent themselves. It was I, the reader, who tended to gloss over the warnings. Finally I learned that I may well be better served in owning 2,000 shares in ten recommended companies as opposed to 20,000 shares in just one of them. It takes a good bit of discipline to remember that the speculation portion of your pyramid is the smallest portion.

A friend of mine asked me recently why a larger percentage of my current investment portfolio seems to be in the area of Casey recommendations. Why is that? I was really glad that question was posed, because it let me step back and analyze... am I putting too many eggs in one basket?

My first explanation came from my concern that inflation – probably hyperinflation – is on the horizon. In today's newspaper there was an article that the US trade deficit came in a couple billion dollars better (less) than what had been forecast. The article went on that a healthier level of US exports was the cause, and then explained that one element of the exports was gold leaving our shores.

MY KIND OF EXPERTS

I explained that the reason so much of my portfolio is in Casey recommendations is that they "get it" better. They understand the inflation hazard that is on my mind. At the same time, there have been recommendations in emerging technologies that I personally felt were pretty cool but decided to pass on. The reason is that I ask myself, "Does this investment seem to be a good one if the economy is going to continue to shrink?" When one is worrying about food on the table, the difference between needs and wants becomes quite clear. The difficulty of satisfying basic needs during a hyperinflation will keep many people – perhaps most – out of the market for the newest, hottest gaming technology.

Then I got put to the real test: Why do you feel the Casey group "gets it" better than some others? Darn good question, and one that will likely change my perspective down the road.

A short time back, one of the newsletters featured an interesting article. It spoke of Warren Buffett and his success and acknowledged that because of his accumulation of wealth he is looked upon as a great investor. The article pointed out that his success over the last few years hasn't been as terrific as it once had been, and it mentioned another issue I had never thought of.

It drew out the difference between an investor, particularly one trained in the colleges and universities, and an economist. Generally, they are versed in the workings of the markets and can read a balance sheet and profit and loss statement and be able to pick out the companies that are good.

On the other hand, the article indicated that many investment newsletters are being written and run by economists. These folks look at the entire world. They look at governments, their laws, rules, and regulations, and see what impact they have on the markets. They are experts at looking at the action of a government and anticipating the economy's reaction and how it will affect society and the investment markets. The more I read, the more I felt the author really did understand and explain the difference.

My conclusion is that I want both! What do I pay the newsletters for… research. I want to know what to expect from the actions of governments around the world, how it is going to affect me and my family, and what action I should take. And yes, that might even be a warning that's time to get while the getting's good! Then from the investment perspective, I want the books of the various companies analyzed to pick the best of the lot.

Using Good Resources

As part of our portfolio is in Do-It-Yourself mode, being managed personally, I have to take the last step and pick and choose the recommendations I believe are the best.

Next up, I'll discuss various alternatives. Time to get the baby its first pair of walking shoes.

Chapter 8

THESE BABY SHOES ARE MADE FOR WALKING

As I started on my Paul Revere crusade to educate my family and friends about the inflation problem which I fear is on the horizon, one central theme became apparent. While some really understood the depth of the potential problem or were at least concerned that indeed inflation could be an issue, the common response was, "Get real!" It took me a while to catch on to what they were trying to tell me as I was inundating them with suggestions.

Most had decent portfolios in the US, but far from what they considered big enough to be handled by a professional money manager. Likely they were friends with their stockbroker and had used the same broker for quite some time. What they wanted to know is what they could do, from their current position, to protect themselves from the ravages of inflation.

After many hours of discussion I came to realize that perhaps I was the one who did not "get it," and I needed to start looking at things from their point of view.

Let's start at the beginning. What are generally the types of investments one can use to hedge against inflation? The ones we investigated fall in to one of the following groups:

1. Precious metals (gold, silver, platinum, *etc.*)

2. Foreign currencies

3. Agricultural land

4. Other collectibles (artwork, coins, *etc.*)

I want to begin by giving an overview of these categories with the vehicles and some specific examples to follow.

PRECIOUS METALS

Precious metals are generally one of the best – if not the best – hedges against hyperinflation. More than one pundit has said, "Gold is real money." Many articles have been written to explain that, and two ways of making the point come to mind.

The first one is simply this: The author looked at the price of a fine man's suit today and also the current price of gold and recalculated the price of the suit. It came to about one ounce of gold. Then he looked at the price of a fine man's suit a hundred years ago and at the price of gold at that time. Then he calculated the century-old price of the suit in gold. Again, the answer was... about one ounce. Gold had held its value over the span of one hundred years, even though the dollar had lost more than 90% of its value.

I saw a similar article centered on a Ford Mustang. They took the price of a Ford Mustang when it appeared on the market in 1964 and calculated the number of one-ounce gold coins it took to buy one. Some 47 years later, the sticker price on the window of the vehicle was much higher; however, it took about the same number of gold pieces to buy the vehicle.

CURRENCIES

Foreign currencies are also considered a hedge against inflation. I read a recent article that said while currencies can be a hedge, there are several factors to consider. When one country is inflating its currency, it takes a lot more of their money to buy a gallon of gas, an ounce of gold, or a bushel of wheat. At the same time, other countries may well also be inflating their currencies, but it's happening at a much slower rate. The key to this investment is to understand which countries are likely to inflate the slowest.

When I took the forex course on learning to trade currencies, it indicated that currencies in countries that had budget surpluses and exported things like gold, silver, or oil were generally the safest – the reason being, for the moment anyway, those commodities are denominated in US dollars. Canada, Norway, and Australia are examples of those types of countries.

LAND

Agricultural land is also a good hedge. In fact, many types of real estate are to some extent. Recently I read that in times of high inflation, the French consider buying a condominium in Paris. My first inclination was they must want a high floor for jumping out from. The author pointed out that they feel that some real estate is considered a "true asset." A friend of mine used to sell real estate and specialized in waterfront property. He liked that because he said they just are not making any more of it these days. I have read recently where, even though the US economy is in quite a slowdown, farmland is seeing an increase in prices. That is quite the opposite of what is happening in the residential market.

COLLECTIBLES

Numismatic coins and other collectibles are supposed to be a good hedge also. Personally, whether it is stamps, coins, or artwork, I know little about them, and they are better left to the experts. The only thing I do know is that the Treasury Department clarified the definition of "collectible" coins, which probably would be less subject to confiscation. The rule was explained to me as this: the value of the coin must be at least 50% higher than the value of the metal. In other words, should gold be selling at $1,800, the value of a coin considered a collectible would have to exceed $2,700.

THE VEHICLES

Now let's take a look at the investment vehicles that give you a stake in inflation hedges. They can be used, many from your kitchen table at home, to begin to protect yourself.

MINING STOCKS

There are many individual gold and silver mining stocks that will generally rise with the inflationary tide. Selecting them requires serious homework and/or help from an expert. That help may come from the right advisor or from a newsletter that specializes in mining stocks.

MUTUAL FUNDS

Next on the docket comes mutual funds. A fund is run by a "fund manager," who picks each investment. If a mutual fund specializes in gold stocks, the manager might buy two dozen or more companies. The idea is diversification, spreading the risk and reward, as opposed to buying stock in just one company.

When you buy into a mutual fund, normally you place the order with fund itself or with a broker to buy the dollar amount you want to invest. At the end of the day, after all the markets close, the fund calculates its "net asset value," which is what one share of the fund is worth, based on the current prices of the fund's investments. They then take the cash you're investing and credit your account with so many shares, usually calculated out to the third decimal place. When you want to sell your shares, you put in your order with the fund or the broker, and your shares are sold at the end of the day for that day's "net asset value."

The fund pays its own expenses, which means that indirectly you and the other investors are paying them. In most cases, the biggest single expense is the fee paid to the manager. It is normally expressed as a percentage of the fund's total net assets. An annual fee of 0.5% of fund assets is about in the middle of the range.

The fund manager has a strong incentive to do well for the investors. Success attracts more investors, which means bigger total assets, which means a bigger total fee for the manager.

EXCHANGE-TRADED FUNDS

An ETF is a hybrid that gives investors many of the advantages of a free-trading stock and many of the advantages of a specialized mutual fund. Most ETFs aren't actively managed the way most mutual funds are. Instead, the typical ETF is committed to a fixed portfolio, for example, all the oil stocks in the Dow Jones average. Some ETFs own just gold bullion. Others own just silver. There are now hundreds of ETFs.

The big difference between a mutual fund and an ETF is that ETF shares are traded all day long, just like regular stocks. With an online brokerage account, you can buy or sell shares in an ETF with a click of a mouse anytime the market is open. The pricing you'll get isn't strictly net asset value, as with a mutual fund trade, but normally the price on your ETF trade will be very close to net asset value.

Mutual funds trade on a daily cycle. ETFs trade from second to second, and sometimes the ability to get in and out quickly can be important. More than one investor watched in horror as events unfolded on 9/11/2001. Knowing that the market was likely to drop as a result, many folks who had mutual funds that specialized in airline stocks put in their sell orders but had to wait until the end of the day on September 17, nearly a week later, to have their trades executed at net asset value for that day. On the other hand, you could have sold your shares in an airline stock ETF before the market was shut down on September 11, which might have cut your losses substantially.

The same would hold true on the upside. In times of crisis, some stocks benefit from the "flight to safety." An event that triggers additional interest in gold can be an opportunity for you to buy – if you buy shares in a gold ETF immediately instead of waiting until the end of the day to buy shares in a mutual fund, after the price has been run up.

FOREIGN EXCHANGE MARKET

The forex market is the where currencies are traded. It is an interesting market, where you can obtain high leverage. Currencies are always traded in pairs, meaning you could make a trade buying Swiss francs against US dollars. In effect you are anticipating that the franc will rise while the dollar will drop.

EVERBANK AND CURRENCIES

EverBank is unique. It offers something much different from renewing a CD in your local bank in US dollars. It provides all the services you would expect from any US bank, and it also allows you to use your dollars to get a certificate of deposit denominated Swiss francs, German marks, Japanese yen, or a range of other currencies. You also can get deposits in currencies from "emerging market" countries and CDs tied to bundles of currencies. All deposits at EverBank, including foreign currency deposits, are covered by FDIC insurance.

My wife has a CD with them in their basket referred to as "New World Energy." It is denominated one-third in Australian dollars, one-third in Canadian dollars, and one-third in Norwegian kroner. The interest rate fluctuates, as it does on dollar CDs, but the real issue is the hedge against inflation. If the US dollar goes down against these currencies, the currency appreciation of the CD could far exceed the interest yield.

Major hint: As I have started to try to educate my friends and family, I have discovered the first baby step usually is a CD from EverBank. It is in the US and is FDIC insured, yet it allows you to get some of your money out of US dollars and into something that can profit from US inflation. One other advantage I found with EverBank is this – every time we have had a foreign currency CD mature, we have rolled it into another CD of the same kind. That's saved us some taxes, because currency gains aren't taxable until you take the money out of the currency. There's an additional advantage we like. One has to go out five to ten years in a traditional CD at a local bank to get their more attractive rates; in today's market, that timeframe is unappealing. At least at present, we like the liquidity advantage of a short-term three-month CD without losing interest.

SPECIFIC INVESTMENTS WE HAVE MADE

I would now like to elaborate on some specific investments we have made in ETFs. I am not endorsing any of the funds, but rather explaining them because they can all be made in the US, and so they are an easy way to get started.

There are ETFs you can invest in that track foreign currencies. A couple of examples includes the Australian Dollar Trust (FXA), which invests in Australian dollars; and Canadian Dollar Trust (FXC), which invests in Canadian dollars.

I just went to my Charles Schwab home page, clicked on the "research" tab, and typed in "FXA." Up popped the information of the opening and closing prices and number of shares traded for the day, just like a regular stock. In addition it indicated that dividends are paid monthly and that the annual yield is 3.79%. The annual dividend yield for FXC (Canada) is 1.84%, paid monthly.

Personally, I did not want to open up a separate forex brokerage account to invest in foreign currencies. That market moves quickly, and you're constantly exposed to margin calls ("put up more money"). I contrast that with my Schwab account. At this moment, FXA is priced over $100/share. If I chose, I could buy 1,000 shares and pay a commission of $8.95 for the trade, just like a regular stock. The dividends go into my Schwab cash account each month, and I would pay the same $8.95 per 1,000 shares when I sell.

Earlier I mentioned the *Currency Capitalist* newsletter. It may well recommend purchasing a certain currency and show how it would be done on the forex market. A couple of times I have read what it has to say and instead made an investment in an ETF for the same currency with good results.

Major baby step: Why complicate things with all the details of the forex market? That's for the true traders. The good ones make a whole lot of money. At the same time, my impression was they are indeed full-time traders, which is a world unto itself. I'm past that stage in life – I consider myself an investor, and the fewer trades I have to make the better. If one is an investor and feels the dollar will go down because of high inflation and the value of the Australian dollar is likely to go up (the country exports gold and oil, among other things), you can buy an ETF right in your stock brokerage account that currently has a yield much higher than most CDs available today.

Bottom line is simple. If you want to hedge, the easy way to do so in currencies is to use an ETF. There are dozens of currency ETFs available. Pick one that matches the currency you want and invest with the click of a mouse or a simple phone call. It works just as easily when you want to sell.

ETFs offer a world of possibilities for those who want to invest in metals. Some funds track the price of gold, some silver, some a combination, others will track junior mining stocks, and some will track major mining companies. The list goes on and on.

As I began to invest in ETFs, I found some wrinkles that need to be pointed out.

Two of the most popular ETFs are GLD (just holds gold) and

SLV (just holds silver). In addition, the Sprott organization has two funds that do about the same thing... almost. PHYS is the symbol for Sprott's gold fund, and PSLV is the symbol for its silver fund.

As a reader of the Ed Steer newsletter *Gold and Silver Daily*, I noticed that he reports the physical metals movement in and out of both GLD and SLV, yet he never mentions the two Sprott funds. I looked into them and discovered the following.

The two Sprott funds are trusts. When the company started the gold funds, it put a certain amount of gold in a vault at the Royal Canadian Mint, which is a Canadian Crown Corporation. To set the initial price of shares in the gold fund, it issued a certain number of fund shares to represent the gold. It took the price per ounce of gold at the time and, based on the number of shares and the number of ounces in the vault, calculated the share price for the first day of issue. The share price from that point forward has varied with the price of gold. Without getting too technical, the company also charges management fees like mutual funds do for administering the fund. As it is a trust, the amount of metal doesn't change; there are no daily flows in and out. In addition, the number of shares outstanding is constant; the company isn't issuing any more.

The Sprott silver fund works the same way.

The Sprott funds do have a physical redemption feature. If your investment is above a certain size, you can request and receive the metal in exchange for your shares and have the bullion shipped anywhere in the world.

What that meant to me is there is real metal backing my investment. It is stored outside the US, hopefully providing some additional protection if the US government ever tries to confiscate gold again.

At the same time, there is one drawback with the Sprott funds. I did an exercise when I was preparing to write this book. The number of shares is limited, and the safety and security those share provide is in high demand. What I did was take the number of ounces of metal they had in storage times the closing price of gold and silver at the end of the day and came up with the total value of metal in the vault. I then took the closing prices of the funds times the number of shares, and it came out to a higher total. At the time PHYS, the gold fund, was garnering a premium of 5.6% over the market value of the gold.

Upon discovering the premium, my initial reaction was to go buy one-ounce gold pieces from a dealer instead. But I that discovered the buyer's premium paid to the dealer was a bit higher than 5.6%. That made the Sprott fund attractive by comparison.

Coins versus Sprott funds isn't an open-and-shut case, however. You have to look at the prices when it's time to buy. At one point, the premium on shares in the silver fund was 21.3% – hardly a bargain at the time.

Compared with GLD and SLV, I personally am more comfortable in the Sprott funds. After reading the reports of the amount of metal flowing in and out of the GLD and SLV, the safety, security, and ultimate inflation protection is what convinced me to use the Canadian alternative.

In addition, there is another interesting fund, CEF, which stands for "Central Fund of Canada." It holds a mix of gold and silver, and its share price has followed the metals very closely.

SOMETHING SIMPLE

Baby step once again: If you want to protect yourself from hyperinflation, there are several easy ways to do so. They include owning gold and silver stocks, ETFs, and owning the physical metal itself. Any and all of these investments can provide some protection if the dollar begins to tank. They are easily bought online or with your broker and can be sold quickly should the fundamentals appear to change and the market turn.

Once again the steps are fairly easy to understand and implement.

1. Look at all the investments you have in your portfolio.

2. Determine which ones would hedge against inflation. Determine which would not protect you against inflation, including investments denominated in US dollars in your brokerage account or in your bank as a CD.

3. Ask yourself if you are comfortable that your current portfolio would hold its value during a sudden surge in inflation... or worse, a hyperinflation. I mentioned in an earlier chapter that the current *Casey Report* suggests 33% in gold and silver, 33% in currencies, and 34% in other. The first 33% – gold and silver – would be excellent hedges to combat inflation.

The next 33% was spread among currencies, so it certainly would afford some protection. Depending on the currencies selected, you indeed would have some sort of hedge.

The final 34% was spread among categories, one being some very selective mining stocks, which could do more than keep up with inflation – they could beat it because of their speculative nature.

4. If you discover that the majority of your portfolio is "at risk" to inflation, then you have many choices available to you. As *The Casey Report* suggested, I would certainly recommend a diversified combination among gold and stocks, currencies, and ETFs directly tied to metals. My experience is that most folks seem comfortable with a CD from EverBank, and they then add different types of investments from that point forward.

5. Dividend-paying stocks are another possible avenue. Inflation of the US dollar is what we are concerned with, and at the moment, I feel the dividend yields on US stocks don't offset inflation. That's why I prefer to invest elsewhere.

So there you have it – safe, easy, and quick ways to get started. CDs from EverBank provide any number of possibilities. You want to spread your exposure to foreign currencies (weve found that ETF's are the easiest and best for us). I really like the monthly dividends that are paid by the Canadian and Australian funds. Gold and silver stocks, as recommended by various investment newsletters, cannot only hedge against inflation but in some cases beat it, particularly when the gold and silver hit what Doug Casey refers to as the Mania Phase. And finally, the investment possibilities in gold and silver ETFs are significant. Choose wisely and you have security, liquidity, and storage outside the country.

It's time for you to get started.

Chapter 9

THE OFFSHORE DECISION

Without a doubt, the most difficult decision my wife and I had to make was dealing with investing offshore. You must first confront the emotional issues. Once you've done that, prepare yourself to be somewhat overwhelmed by the "how" side of the decision. The rules, regulations, and choices are expansive, which is really good because if you do make the "go" decision, you then can tailor a plan that's comfortable.

I want to touch on the emotional issues first, because they are big. For me they were difficult, because I had no idea just how ingrained some of my beliefs were.

At one point in my life, my oldest daughter was in her late 20s and was a vice president of a large, well-known bank, with several hundred people in her department. At a family gathering, we were discussing a controversial issue about how the world is changing around us, and she said something to the effect, "Dad, I don't think it is a matter of things you have to learn as much as it is things you need to unlearn!" In retrospect, truer words were never spoken. It just took me a decade or more to understand what she was saying.

From my days as a young boy, I remember the war bonds. I remember a school bond drive and a teacher holding up a bond and having us read, "The full faith and credit of the United States of America," with the implication that the bond was "good as gold."

The Offshore Decision

Not too many years ago, I attended my high-school class'
50th reunion. Of course, the yearbooks were set out, and the
valedictorian, the student most likely to succeed, and those with
athletic and academic honors were recognized. I told my wife not
to bother looking – she won't find my name or photo on any of
those pages.

As we sat with our group at the nice, round table for the
banquet, we obviously were reliving events of many years ago.
I finally blurted out to the folks at the table that they should be
thanking guys like me, for we're the ones who made the upper
half of the class possible. After a good laugh, I told the table that
I should have won the efficiency award. Someone took the bait
and said they had never heard of that. I explained that I probably
got the highest grades for the least amount of effort of anyone in
our graduating class. I just never found school interesting.

Then I recounted an event that could be called "something
no one would ever remember but you will never forget." For us
to graduate from high school, we had to study and pass a pretty
extensive test on both the state and US Constitutions. It was
about much more than simply what was written. It was how
about how the Constitution was designed, how it worked, the
checks and balances, and what it was intended to do.

When all had taken the test, all had passed, so all would
graduate. I was sitting in the front row when the government
teacher announced that I had scored the highest grade in the
class. There was a long pause and some surprise, but the unsaid
implication was that I was either lucky or cheated. Nothing could
have been further from the truth.

Sometime later I decided to define a couple of terms as they affected me. I would define "studying" as the art of trying to stay awake while reading something totally boring, about a subject you had no interest it, with the goal of passing a test on Friday so you would not have to repeat the course.

I would define "research" as finding something you are truly interested in, voluntarily gathering as much data as you could to learn about it, perhaps reading about it well into the night because it is fun and interesting. For some reason that assignment on learning about the Constitution and government was one of the first things in my life that I really found interesting. (Now, for my classmates, I also must add "other than girls or sports," but you get the picture.)

SOMETHING LOST

For years I believed and preached to my children that the Constitution is what separated the United States from every other nation on earth. It is what has allowed us to prosper. In a period of 200 years, the improvements the US has brought to mankind all over the world surpassed the sum total of all of those things accomplished prior to 1776. Indeed, I was one who was mentally wrapped in the American flag, baseball, hot dogs, apple pie. and Chevrolet.

Couple that background forming my core belief with government propaganda that anyone who has money offshore is either a member of the mafia or a drug cartel or is sending money offshore to evade taxes, I was an individual with a core belief with cement wrapped around it like that shielding a nuclear reactor.

I recall reading that Doug Casey said you should be a citizen of one country, live in another country, and have money in a third country. My reaction was that it was easy to say for a man who has travelled the world his entire life and perhaps speaks more than one language.

Shortly after I began subscribing to investment newsletters, I recall David Galland mentioning the effects of inflation. He told the story about being on a conference call with several folks who all were worth $20 million or more. They then calculated that even if inflation was a mere 5% they would lose $1 million in personal buying power. My reaction was, "Geesh, I really feel sorry, you guys only have $19 million left. What about us real people?"

In essence, since I wasn't a wealthy world traveler, the idea of investing offshore frankly did not apply to me or my family.

As I mentioned, years earlier I had subscribed to many investment newsletters and was also a member of the Sovereign Society. Occasionally it would run articles about investing offshore, and the first few paragraphs would be why one would consider it, then it would be followed with pages regarding offshore trusts, basically outlining vehicles you would use to invest offshore and then the type of investments you could make. Honestly, if one is not sold on the idea in the first place, then the portion after the first few paragraphs was of little interest.

FOCUS ON WHY

Today my first suggestion on this subject would be: **Focus only on the issue of why would you consider investing offshore.** If you've found articles on the subject, take a pair of scissors and cut the paper after the last sentence on why and put it in the "why" stack, and then the rest should be put in the "how" stack.

I suggest you start by asking yourself some pretty basic questions.

1. Do you trust the US government?

2. Do you trust the US government not to make decisions that could harm you or your family financially?

3. If there were a dispute between you and the IRS, would the IRS play fair?

4. Are there some investment vehicles available only outside the United States that would help you meet your investment objectives? Vehicles that could indeed help you offset hyperinflation?

Suggestion #2: **Don't bunch your decisions or decision-making process.** My wife and I have thought the situation over and discussed it at length many times. The United States is the country people come to with "their little bag of gold." At least so far, it's not the country where people leave with the clothes on their back and gold stuffed wherever they can hide it. Our children and grandchildren are here. This is our home. As bad as we may feel our government is, there is still no place on earth we

111

would rather be... for the moment. In other words, *the discussion is not whether **you** want to move offshore; that is a separate issue entirely. The first issue to deal with is only whether you want to move **part of your money** offshore.*

I can tell folks how we felt about the four questions I mentioned. You and your family may well feel differently, but here is what we concluded.

DO WE TRUST THE GOVERNMENT?

Our best answer was, **"Toto, we're not in Kansas anymore."** Trust the government... not anymore, or at least not with the blind faith and allegiance that we used to feel. For me personally, I suspect this is when the bloom came off the rose and my daughter's wisdom came into play. I was personally having to rethink some core beliefs that had been ingrained into my mind as a child.

I have told many young folks to ask their parents or grandparents about life in the early 1950s. Many bought their first car and never took the keys out, would park in a lot with the windows down, go into a store, and the keys remained in the ignition. Ask if they ever locked their front door, and most will say only if they were going to be on vacation for a couple of weeks. It was a much different America than it is today. Of course society has changed, and the government has also changed. Life was a lot more like Andy Griffith's, the fictional sheriff of Mayberry, North Carolina, in the television show than young people realize. But those days are gone, nothing but a nice memory.

The Offshore Decision

The first realization was that our current situation is not the result of one political party. George Bush campaigned as a fiscal conservative but certainly did not govern that way. Our current president campaigned on being totally transparent, even making a campaign promise that all bills before Congress would be posted on the internet for 24 to 48 hours before they would be put to a vote. Not 24 months later, I watched an interview with the Speaker of the House as she was being asked about the healthcare bill. She responded that, "I guess you will have to pass it to find out what's in it!" – and she was totally serious. I am sure I am not the only person who looked at the television and had trouble believing what I was seeing.

This issue of trusting the government in America is fundamental. I watched in horror as I saw videos on TV of Black Panther members, dressed in combat gear with billy clubs in their hands intimidating voters at the polls. The story included the fact that the Justice Department decided to drop the case and not prosecute it. We mentioned it to some of our friends who had not seen the newscast and they basically said, "Not in America," that could never happen in the United States. They thought that I was making it up.

I have selected the above cases not to try to sell my particular point of view, but rather to try to force us all to get out of our comfort zone and become aware of what is going on around us.

Earlier I mentioned that in the early 1930s the government basically confiscated all the gold coins that the citizens of the country had in their possession. That certainly hurt a lot of Americans, as the dollars they received for their gold lost 75% of their value. I would imagine that anyone who owned gold likely felt betrayed by their government. Personally, I would much prefer to have sold my gold after it was revalued, not before; that's why we buy it to begin with, to keep up with inflation.

COULD OR WOULD THE GOVERNMENT MAKE DECISIONS THAT COULD HARM OUR FAMILY?

About the time we were faced with the offshore decision, I had read where the US was having difficulty borrowing money. The idea came up of raiding everyone's IRA and forcing them to liquidate all their investments and replace them with government bonds. The article I read also said that Argentina had just done that very thing.

That hit much too close to home, as the bulk of our investment capital is in my IRA. It was then that I realized what would really happen if they tried to do that. First of all, the amount of net worth in my IRA would probably drop by 50% or more. Can you imagine if every IRA in America put in sell orders for their investments at the same time? Who would buy them? To me it seemed that the investment crash of 1929 would be tame by comparison. Then, with what little I had left, I would be forced to buy worthless IOUs from a government already bankrupt. Now that hit too close to home.

DO YOU FEEL THE IRS WOULD PLAY FAIR?

For the last 35 years I have used a CPA to prepare our taxes... same company, as a matter of fact, first the father and now his son. Compliance with the tax code has been the system we believe in. It was a simple matter of practicality. During my working career I spent a significant amount of time on the road. Were I to have to appear before the IRS, that would mean I was taken out of business for that time because my clients paid me by the day. Better to comply. The one time we were audited by the IRS, I was able to have my CPA represent me; the IRS asked for the data, we provided them with that data, and that was it.

When I read horror stories about the IRS being able to freeze anyone's personal assets and bank accounts, it certainly strikes fear in my heart. Better to just comply. That is probably what IRS standard procedures are intended to do. Personally, based on exactly that one experience, I would have said the IRS was fair.

However, in the mid 1980s I divorced, moved from Atlanta to Fort Myers, Florida, and found myself starting life over in many ways. I traveled for work 90% of the time, so basically I was only in Fort Myers on weekends.

I quickly learned that I share a name with another person in town. He didn't pay his bills, and I was soon inundated with phone calls and letters from collection agencies. Once the sheriff even tried to serve a summons – mercifully, I was out of town.

On one occasion I got a call from a casino in San Juan about an unpaid gambling debt and found myself trying to explain that they'd called the wrong person. Of course, I had a mental picture of some mafia collection agent, barely able to speak English, banging on my front door holding a violin case demanding payment. Fortunately that did not happen.

The Offshore Decision

The most intimidating call, however, came in from the IRS. They demanded that I call them immediately at a specific 800 number, which I immediately did, but uh oh! I was in Colorado at the time, and the number had to be called from the state of Florida; I wouldn't be there on a weekday for six weeks.

At that point, I had been dating for exactly one week the lady who would eventually become my bride. I had no one else in Florida I could call for help. I waited until my lunch break, took a deep breath, and called her to explain the situation. I gave her my Social Security Number and asked her to call the IRS and explain that they were bugging the wrong man. Of course, there was a long pause as I suspect she wondered what kind of deadbeat she had gone out with last weekend. But she made the call and said the IRS lady was pretty aggressive until she finally checked my Social Security Number. The lady then said something like, "Oh, okay," but didn't apologize for her harassment.

For the next six months or so, I must admit that I don't know who I was more concerned about possibly banging on my door – a collection agent from a San Juan casino or the IRS. When I hear commercials from attorneys claiming the IRS is the most ruthless collection agent on the planet, I have a tendency to agree with them. But I don't want to ever find out.

When the government is spending 40% more than it is taking in and politicians are worried about their jobs, one would have to assume their collection agency – which can quickly tie up one's assets in a dispute – is no one to mess with.

One more layer of my core belief peeled away, one more thing for me to unlearn.

ARE THERE OFFSHORE INVESTMENT VEHICLES AVAILABLE TO HELP US MEET OUR OBJECTIVES THAT ARE NOT AVAILABLE IN THE UNITED STATES?

At the time we made the decision to investigate further, the answer would have been that we did not know. In retrospect, someone may have told me that there were important opportunities offshore, but I likely would not have understood them at the time.

Today my answer is a most emphatic "yes." And that's the result of having taken a large portion of my IRA offshore and having seen and learned of things I never before knew existed.

One very quick example would be this. One of the first investments that René Schatt (WHVP) made was to buy shares of the company Silver Wheaton on the Canadian Stock Exchange. Now, that stock is also available on a US stock exchange. At the time I wondered why he bought it in Canada instead. Luckily he timed it well, and in a two-year period the stock quadrupled. Now, it also did the same on the US exchange. Following the Casey Research model, René decided to sell off a portion – to use the slang phrase, to take his money off the table. Now the remainder of the investment was profits invested as a result of appreciation. It was when I was trying to make the entry on my Quicken program to keep track of things that I realized something: not only had the stock quadrupled, but also the value of the Canadian dollar had gone up by 16% vs. the US dollar over the same period. Wow! That had never happened to me before.

Over the last few years we have had regular quarterly conference calls. I have come to the realization that the international folks think totally differently from most brokers in the United States. I want them to teach me how they think.

My daughter was right – I had much to unlearn. The decision as to whether we should send money offshore to be managed by a person we never met, halfway around the world, was likely the most emotionally difficult decision we had to make. For us, it was one of the best decisions we made. Personally, we are staying here... for the moment; but we are quite comfortable with our money being somewhere else.

EXPLORING THE BIG WORLD

Should you conclude, as we did, that offshore investing with part of your money offers more protection than having it all in the US, you will find many useful tools. I mentioned the Sovereign Society, because they have lots of articles and even workshops on the why and how to go about the process. The Casey group and Sprott Investments offer some excellent guidance also. And for free you can tap a powerful resource for offshore investing by signing up as a member of InternationalMan.com.

The Offshore Decision

In the early stages I was quite confused as to the correct process. For example, if you are sending money from your IRA offshore, the process is different than if you're sending personal funds. When transmitting IRA funds offshore, we had to use an IRA custodian in the US that WHVP works with. Our money was wired from my IRA's US brokerage account to the new IRA custodian in the US, then to the offshore bank holding the account under the name of my IRA. Once there, management by WHVP begins.

The best way to get started is to talk with those who handle US clients; they are very familiar with the law and the proper steps to move your IRA money legally to other parts of the world. I must confess I used to think it would be illegal to have IRA money invested offshore. That is not the case at all; you just have to make sure you do it in the manner that follows the rules.

Earlier we discussed the decision to use an advisor or go the do-it-yourself route. In our case we chose to do both.

When we came to understand the idea of "core holdings" and the added protection of storing precious metals offshore, the idea of Perth Mint Certificates really appealed to us. Their US representative is Asset Strategies International in Maryland, where Glenn Kirsch was a partner. The company actually worked with the Perth Mint to design the program for US investors. As those assets were purchased out of our personal funds, we did not need to use our IRA custodian.

If one prefers to have some gold or silver closer to home, the Sprott Investments group has some programs available also.

The Offshore Decision

In summary, my suggestions would be to unbundle the decision process. You have many separate decisions that should be looked at independently:

1. Would you be better off protecting your assets by having all or a portion of them invested offshore?

2. Is moving offshore in times of crisis a realistic option at this point in your life? I will readily admit that my wife and I have said on several occasions, were I in my 50s instead of my 70s, likely we would have a second home offshore. In addition, we have investigated the moving offshore issue in depth. We attended three International Living conferences, two in foreign countries. Should the situation here in the US become intolerable for us, we do have a contingency plan in place... much like a fire extinguisher, we hope we never have to activate it.

3. From what accounts will I take funds to move offshore? That will lead to understanding the proper process for doing so. The decision to send IRA money was driven partly by the article I read about the US government thinking of doing as Argentina has done, requiring retirement accounts to be invested in government bonds. We do not find that idea appealing at all.

4. How much can we afford to invest offshore? In our case, we estimated the earnings in our other accounts plus the amount of our IRAs remaining in the US should be enough to support use for at least seven years. After that, hopefully the offshore accounts will have grown to the point where

we can withdraw a portion of each year's current earnings, couple it with our Social Security, and be able to live comfortably for the rest of our lives.

5. What to invest in? This could lead to hundreds if not thousands of possibilities. In our case we decided to use a money manager, which has been a terrific experience for us. Our knowledge base about international investing is growing by the day. This is a result of the subscription services we read regularly, coupled with hands-on experience in watching and learning from our money manager.

OFFSHORE BLOCKS IN YOUR PYRAMID

After I had developed the investment pyramid as outlined earlier, I discovered that I had many different ways to fill in each layer on the pyramid. For example, our Perth Mint Certificates plus some small holdings in coins, work well in the base-level, core holdings. WHVP is by design very conservative, and as a result my IRA funds offshore will not invest in anything speculative. Then, between my accounts and my wife's accounts here in the US, we fill in the areas of the pyramid where we feel further allocation is necessary. For example, in my wife's account are CDs at EverBank denominated in foreign currencies. At the same time, we have exposure to some of the more speculative recommendations in *The Casey Report*, *Casey International Speculator,* and *BIG GOLD*.

I mentioned earlier that I use Quicken to keep track of all our investment accounts, including the offshore accounts. With the click of a mouse, we have an excellent idea of where we are in total each and every day. Quicken will update most of it automatically, and some I do manually (probably because I do not know how to program it into Quicken properly).

Recently some of our closest friends have come to us with questions. One comment my wife made to me is that I tend to speak with a good deal of confidence. Well, it was a little over two years ago that the proper description of my state was "scared and for good reason." I also have realized that, because my entire portfolio had turned into a pile of cash, we had to jump into the water with both feet. That is not what I would recommend to anyone. Start with baby steps – investments you are comfortable with. Then challenge yourself to continue to become educated until you are comfortable with a second step.

An important rule is this: **You must understand *why* you are doing something differently than what you have done in the past. Second, you need to understand the investment you are going into.** For the investments that I chose to manage myself, both requirements were easy to satisfy. Should you decide to have an advisor help you, then you must have faith and trust in his judgment. Once he has purchased an investment in your name, do not be shy in inquiring and learning about not only the investment but why he chose it. I promise you a good education will quickly become part of the process.

FALSE IMAGE

Back in the early 1970s, I made my first business trip to Bermuda. I got into a taxicab and learned the hotel was on the other side of the island, some 16 miles away. The taxi driver asked me where I was from and I said, "Chicago." He literally turned around to look at me in the back seat, took his hands as though he were operating a Tommy Gun and went, "D-d-d-d-dah DOW!" pretending he was shooting. It provided a good laugh, but then I proceeded to educate him that the famous St. Valentine's Day massacre had occurred over 50 years ago and, while Chicago had quite a reputation, it was not as dangerous a place to live as he might think.

It really turned out to be an interesting conversation, as he told me about what he reads in the paper. And from what he was exposed to in the media, I could understand how he might have felt that Chicago was just as violent as it was during the gangland wars of the Prohibition era. At the very least, the constant drumbeat from what he read and saw on television was what fed his beliefs.

As I prepared this book, reviewing and reliving our experiences in my mind, I realized that I was no different than the taxi driver in formulating my feelings about investing offshore. Today, as much as any time in my life, we are constantly bombarded with the "rich with their offshore tax havens" being totally reinforced by the media trying to influence public opinion. Now I have come to believe that the more the government trumpets this tune, the more it reinforces the need for a prudent investor to protect himself.

After attending several conferences over the last couple years, to use my daughter's term, I have "unlearned" a lot. Most of the people I met were just hard-working folks concerned about looking after their families now and into the future. If anything, they bend over backward to make sure they comply with the law.

The Offshore Decision

I read an article in one of the newsletters that dealt with compliance with the IRS regulations on offshore investing and the various forms that need to be completed. One of the issues I came upon was that if you have a traditional IRA offshore, certain forms are necessary. If, however, you have a Roth IRA, then a different set of reports are required. Wanting to be 100% sure, I decided hearing it from a second source would be nice. I dropped David Galland from Casey Research an email and asked if he had heard this information. His response to me was simple: "Report it anyway. When it comes to this sort of thing you cannot be too careful." To which I say, "Amen to that; I agree," but I would also add, "Don't let fear keep you from legally protecting your life's work accumulated in savings."

Our journey has taken us to where we are really a hybrid. A certain portion of our investments are in the US, in our brokerage account, and with EverBank. We manage those ourselves; it is fun, and so far we are doing just fine. At the same time a major portion is also offshore, being managed by a professional. Between the US and offshore investments, I see my job as to make sure each level of our investment pyramid is all filled with assets we are comfortable with.

I just took a peek at our Quicken file, and we are currently invested in eight different currencies, including US dollars, numerous ETFs (both in foreign currencies and metals), plus some individual stocks. Offshore are additional investments in stocks on foreign exchanges and some high-rated bonds, primarily from solid countries and all in foreign currencies. It kind of boggles my mind to think how far we have come in just three years.

I am not inclined to think we have it all figured out by any means. Inflation will pass, hopefully with minimal damage to our country, and then there will be new challenges. The first will be much like when our CDs got called in. We will be moving out of inflation hedges and into cash while we trying to figure out what lies ahead. I wonder what our Quicken file will look like in ten years.

I read daily because I want to know what is going on in the world. My wife reads much of what I do also. I will be on constant alert, looking for the clues and tidbits from one of the investment gurus signaling that the fundamentals are likely to change, so I can beat the crowd out of our inflation investments and hold on to as much profit possible. We're taking care of business, but we still have plenty of time for fun and the things we enjoy. It's not nearly as overwhelming as we once thought. We look forward with the confidence that whatever comes our way – much like the first time I ran three miles without stopping – we will be ahead of many and looking to those who are far more advanced than we are to help keep us on the right road.

The last three years have taught me several things. I realize that no one will care as much about my money as I do. As a retiree, my goal is to stay healthy and retired and have fun in the process. To succeed, I can't let myself get lazy; staying on top of things and protecting our life savings is what is going to help us maintain our health and hopefully allow for a lot of fun things in our golden years.

Even though we may not be able to see over the crest of the next hill, we can be confident that we have come this far and we will be equipped to handle what lies ahead.

Chapter 10

WRAPPING THINGS UP

In Doug Casey's presentation at the *When Money Dies* Conference in Phoenix, he defined government as "a monopoly of power in a given geographical area." The more I thought about it, the more I agreed. Try committing a crime or avoiding paying what they say is your share of taxes and you will see just how powerful they can be.

He went on to explain that there are three legitimate purposes of government. The first is to protect us from harm from enemies outside our borders. The second is to protect us from harm from within our borders. The third is to provide a judicial system, so that you don't have to resort to violence when you have a disagreement with another citizen. Makes sense to me.

As a person on the leading edge of the baby boomers, for the most part the government seems to have been doing a fairly decent job of all three for much of my lifetime. While we can all rightfully complain about the infringements upon our freedom, for the most part we have been able to work for a living, raise a family, and go about our business as long as we lived within the rules.

Still, we see changes taking place around us all the time, and many of them make us uncomfortable. Things seem to be happening that a decade ago would have been unimaginable. One of the changes that bothers a lot of senior citizens is a major shift in attitude. Let me explain.

THE ELEPHANT IN YOUR CHAIR

I have a close friend who is a true big-game hunter. He goes on real safaris in Africa and hunts big game once or twice a year, and the guide really does call him "Bwana." He tells me the rules for a safari are quite rigid. He goes to a particular country in Africa and has to buy a hunting permit, much like folks in our country who have to get a license to hunt or fish. In his case, however, it is much more restrictive and very expensive.

A few years back, he got a permit to hunt an elephant. The permit gave him a legal right to hunt for one elephant in a particular geographic area for a particular period of time, like a month maximum. Should he come across a pride of lions, unless his life is really threatened, he best leave them alone; otherwise he could end up in a very hot prison. Now, he has gone on many safaris where they hunted for days and didn't spot the particular type of animal for which he had a permit. He could spend $30,000 for a long walk in the woods and come home empty-handed.

When he got home from one trip, he was very excited. He had found and shot his elephant. Now, I am not a hunter; and I am married to a real animal lover. I made the mistake of going with my wife to a cat show once and learned one does not walk around looking at cats; one must go and talk to every cat in the show in every cage. Well, my wife was more than uneasy and asked his wife how she deals with the idea of her husband shooting an elephant. She explained to my wife that no matter what animal they hunt, they are required to harvest the meat, and that particular elephant fed an entire tribe for almost a month.

Wrapping Things Up

As he was showing me his photos, I saw a picture of the herd and asked him how he picked out a particular target. He said that they are required to find an aging male, normally walking much slower at the back of the herd. I made the mistake of asking him, "Why is that?" He responded that the aging male is of no value to the herd.

Hey, wait a minute! I'm an aging male, in my 70s, with my first great-grandchild now here, and yeah, I walk a bit slower these days. He jokingly said that if I were an elephant, I would be a target. He then went on to explain that in Africa you can be sure the aging citizens are the ones who are the easiest for the lions to pick off, too. Throughout history, growing older has meant becoming vulnerable and becoming a target for the strong and the swift.

For me, what my friend said hit much too close to home. Let's take notice.

How many articles have we seen recently where the author is talking about budget deficits and government spending and outlining the **problem** they are going to have when all the Baby Boomers are on Social Security? In essence, the Baby Boomers are no longer productive citizens, and Social Security makes them a burden on the younger generation.

During the Carter administration the country had terrible inflation, and to protect seniors Congress passed a law indexing Social Security to inflation. Now that many citizens are getting closer to retirement, it has changed the rules for calculating inflation, to cut what they'll have to pay in Social Security.

How many more times are we going to hear the radio and television blaring with politicians screaming that the rich don't pay their fair share? While they may talk about high income earners, make no mistake: "rich" is anyone who has managed to accumulate any kind of wealth.

Recently I saw where the government was talking about some sort of "wealth tax" to help reduce the budget deficit. What a joke that is. When was the last time the government took in tax dollars and paid off any part of its debt... as opposed to finding some new program to waste the money on? Clue: I think it was in the late 1940s, when Truman was president. Ummm, yeah – when our generation was just getting started.

It all tied together for me when I read a newsletter recently discussing the rise and fall of many governments over the years. The author said governments get desperate and will do almost anything to hang on to their power. ***Indeed, I realized that the government is the hunter and those folks with any kind of wealth, particularly seniors, are the hunted.***

Sure I want to scream. Hey, we bought into your Social Security scheme! Heck, I paid into the system for over 55 years personally. We lived by the rules, worked our tails off, and saved our money. We all tried to be like the squirrel that stores enough nuts to last as long as he lives.

We are not the problem: the government is the problem. When we started working, there was a real, honest-to-God Social Security trust fund. It was the government that chose to raid the fund to pay for stupid spending programs that did not work. It filled the trust fund with IOUs that will be coming due big-time over the next decade as the Baby Boomers retire. Why is it that **we** are now the problem?

I know a good number of senior citizens who will tell you their favorite song is by Frank Sinatra; part of the chorus goes, "I did it my way."

If you have read this far, there is a good chance that you too have worked doggone hard and been fortunate to accumulate some decent savings so you can enjoy the rest of your life and not become a financial burden on society or your children.

What I have tried to outline in this book is pretty simple. Wake up and look around – is there any kind of threat to your life savings, which in turn can affect your lifestyle for the rest of your life? You know how I feel about that question.

Then I tried to quantify the risk, to put it into terms we can all understand and relate to.

The next step was to help people understand that things are not much different than they were when we working our tails off 50-80 hours a week for decades on end. I say that with confidence, because I know absolutely no one who has accumulated even modest wealth who did not do so by working a whole lot more than 40 hours a week. During those years, we had to look out for ourselves and protect our families. Nothing has changed, except that the adverse consequences of not doing so are now much greater. Screw up in our 40s and you get a do-over. I literally started over financially at the age of 47 and had to work pretty hard to catch up, but I was grateful that I was young enough to be able to do it.

Unless you believe in reincarnation, life is not so forgiving as to allow seniors that same do-over opportunity.

Here is the beauty. Once we have our life savings, our nest egg if you will, we do not have to protect it by having a strong back and large muscles. We can protect it by using our minds and making good decisions. We have the benefit of making many mistakes over decades, and hopefully that gives us wisdom. Likely we have more tools available to us, particularly on the computer, than ever before in the history of man.

My purpose in this book is to try to help folks realize what we realized: there are a whole lot of really bad things that could easily happen that could destroy your life savings in less than a month. There is a government doing everything it can to make it difficult for us to make good investment choices. Recently I had a friend say that he looked into giving up his US citizenship. Basically he told me he was free to leave the country but the government would basically tax him as though he died. **In other words, it is not really his money – it is the government's money, and he is the temporary custodian.** A desperate government is not willing to wait; they are like the spoiled child who wants it now.

Once we come to the hard realization about the challenges in front of us, then what should we do? Our journey was one of learning. While I'm sure I could not run even a mile today, I am still capable of reading for several hours a day if necessary. *It*

is education and knowledge that will be the tool and salvation of the investor.

After we discussed and fully understood what could and likely will happen, we discussed many steps and alternatives you can take to protect your investments. As I look back, many are pretty easy steps and can be done with the click of a mouse on your computer. It is just a matter of taking a little time to learn and then taking each step one at a time, at whatever speed makes you comfortable. There are good folks out there who can help; it's just a matter of finding them, but it can be done.

One thing most seniors will tell you is they are very much aware of their mortality; we have a lot more life behind us than left in front of us.

On the other hand, I have mentioned one of my favorite Doug Casey quotes: "Just because something is inevitable does not mean it is imminent." I want to meld that with another of my favorite quotes. This is by the author James Michener and is from _The Fires of Spring_:

"For this is the journey that men make, to find themselves. It doesn't matter what else they find, fame, fortune, many loves, revenge, when the tickets are collected at the end of the ride they are tossed in the bin marked failure. But if a man happens to find himself, the extent of his courage, the limit of his dedication, the position in life from which he will no longer retreat, he has found a mansion he can inhabit with dignity all the days of his life."

Many young folks do not understand that is what the Sinatra

song *My Way* is really all about. While we know what is inevitable, we have worked hard to accumulate our life saving so we can enjoy the rest of the ride, and we want to enjoy it with dignity for as long as we can. We worked hard so that when the inevitable and imminent day finally comes, together we can say we did it our way.

DISCLOSURE STATEMENT

At this point, I feel it necessary to follow the advice of a dear friend who helped proofread this material. She suggested that I insert a "full disclosure statement" so those reading this material do not find themselves preoccupied, wondering about my personal motivation in discussing various sources and companies we have chosen to do business with. That made sense to me.

Many years ago there was a very popular television show call *Dragnet*. It was a show that outlined crimes being committed, and then the good-guy cops would find a way to solve the mystery shortly before the last commercial break. They opened each show with a statement that "The story you are about to see is true. The names have been changed to protect the innocent."

In my case, it is a bit different. The cases are true; however, the mystery is not solved. You are reading about my experiences, frustrations, fears, and lessons I've learned and are still learning along the way. Unlike the television show, when I name a company I've done business with, a particular newsletter, or name a particular individual, they are real. Should I not want to name a particular individual, I simply refer to him as a friend.

In addition, while I've shared names of people, newsletters, and in some cases companies, these mentions should not be considered as any type of endorsement. And as I told my "dear friend" who made the suggestion of the disclosure statement, I have no financial motivation to guide any reader to use their services. There are no commissions, referral fees, nor other "cuts."

I feel a need to make one other personal point. Glen Kirsch was responsible for guiding me into many of the services and companies I currently work with today. At the time he gave me his help, I was not aware that companies and services like that were available. For example, we now use a firm, Weber Hartmann Vrijhof & Partners (WHVP), which just a few years back I hadn't heard of. In fact, I didn't realize companies like this even existed. It was not until I attended the Money Show in Orlando that I discovered there were many companies that do what they do and do it well. Before I spoke with Glen, I would not have even known what to look for in the Yellow Pages or on the Internet to try and find that kind of help.

Epilogue

MILLER'S MONEY WEEKLY

Thank you for reading *Retirement Reboot*.

It's my sincere hope that you now have the confidence and tools to more actively manage your retirement finances. I didn't set out in 2008 to take over management of my retirement, but the changes thrust upon us compelled me to. Everything we learned in the past about managing our retirement money has changed, and like it or not, we're all money managers now.

I suggest that as you're assessing your own retirement strategy, you should consult the book from time to time on how I overcame certain challenges. I'm not saying my way is the right answer for everyone, but you can use my ideas as a starting point for developing your own plan.

And the changes you're putting in place right now will need to be continually monitored and revised. This isn't something you can put on autopilot, but it doesn't need to be time consuming either. We've seen how events and conditions of just the past few years have forced us to make significant changes to managing our retirement finances; and I see no indication that the future won't require us to be just as adaptive.

Retirement Reboot is the start to you taking a more active role in managing your retirement money, but it's just the start. Market conditions, government regulations, the economy – they all change, and you'll need new insights, strategies, and ideas to adapt and thrive.

That's why even before *Retirement Reboot* was published I started a newsletter called ***Miller's Money Weekly***.

With ***Miller's Money Weekly***, I bring you insights and analysis on market trends and financial matters relevant to our group – retirees and near-retirees – in my usual frank and personal matter, based on my own personal experiences and the investment expertise of the Casey Research team. We've recently covered articles with headlines like *The Greatest Investment I Ever Made*, *Twelve Tips for Buying Dividend-Paying Stocks*, and *"We Buy Gold"*. With these articles and others like them delivered to your inbox every week, you'll be able to put into practice even more of the lessons from this book.

Some other key topics I've recently covered:

- The financial impact of a second marriage
- Understanding how to use stop losses
- Investing in technology with little risk
- Evaluating the risks and potential impact of inflation
- Calculating your insurance coverage needs

And each issue is backed by the financial analysts at Casey Research, one of the most highly respected investment-research firms in America!

Don't let another day go by without taking steps to secure your retirement: you're the one who has the most at stake. Start by signing up for my free newsletter, ***Miller's Money Weekly***. Simply visit www.millersmoney.com/reboot-owner to sign up today and see past issues.

Dennis Miller

GLOSSARY OF ACRONYMS AND REFERENCES

ASI   Asset Strategies International. This is where it all started, with a phone call to the late Glen Kirsch. www.assetstrategies.com

CD   Certificate of Deposit. Normally the name of the document an investor receives when he chooses to lend money to a bank. In the US, most are federally insured up to $250,000.

CFP   Certified Financial Planner. This is a designation that financial people earn through taking a series of courses about financial planning and then passing a very comprehensive test.

ECB   European Central Bank. This organization is similar to the Federal Reserve in the United States. While most countries have a central bank, the ECB is the central bank for the 17 countries that make up the Eurozone. The currency is the euro.

ETF   Exchange-Traded Fund. This is a type of investment which is similar to a mutual fund but trades like a stock. They vary in scope to include different markets, metals, currencies, and any number of other investment groupings. They offer an excellent alternative to people who want to combat inflation through foreign currencies or precious metals.

Glossary

EverBank.   The US bank that offers unique investment
opportunities in foreign currencies and metals,
many insured by the FDIC. www.everbank.com

FDIC   Federal Deposit Insurance Corporation. The agency of the
federal government that insures deposits in US banks.

FX   A market where currencies are traded. www.forex.com

GLD   The symbol for a particular ETF that tracks the price of
gold. The technical name is SPDR Gold Trust.

PHYS   The trading symbol for the Sprott ETF dealing with gold.
The technical name is Sprott Physical Gold Trust. Its gold
is stored in the Royal Canadian Mint.

SLV   The symbol for a particular ETF that tracks the price of
silver. The technical name is IShares Silver Trust.

TARP   Troubled Asset Relief Program. Congress authorized this
on October 3, 2008, to bail out banks that were in trouble
because of the subprime mortgage crisis. The government
authorized $700 billion, and the last information
available indicated they had released close to $500 billion
from the authorized amount.

WHVP   Weber Hartmann Vrijhof & Partners. An independent
financial services firm located in Zurich, Switzerland.
www.whvp.ch